Aging Solo

A Single Woman's Guide To Creating A Confident Future

Ellen Dawson

Daisy-Publishing, LLC

Copyright © 2024 by Ellen Dawson

Legal Notice:

All rights reserved.

No portion of this book may be reproduced in any form without written permission from the publisher or author, except as permitted by U.S. copyright law.

This book is only for personal use. Content cannot be amended, distributed or sold without the consent of the author or publisher.

Under no circumstances will any blame or legal responsibility be held against the publisher, or author, for any damages, reparation, or monetary loss due to the information contained within this book. Either directly or indirectly.

Disclaimer Notice:

Please note the information contained within this document is for educational and entertainment purposes only. All effort has been expended to present accurate, up-to-date, and reliable, complete information. No warranties of any kind are declared or implied. Readers acknowledge that the author is not engaging in the rendering of legal, financial, medical, or professional advice. The content within this book has been derived from various sources.

By reading this document, the reader agrees that under no circumstances is the author responsible for any losses, direct or indirect, which are incurred as a result of the use of the information contained within this document, including, but not limited to, — errors, omissions, or inaccuracies.

Contents

INTRODUCTION ... 1

CHAPTER 1 ... 7
Embrace the Challenge - Living Solo
    What Are We Afraid of?
    Just the Facts, Ma'am!
    Retirement

CHAPTER 2 ... 25
Manage Money Mindfully - Welcome Desires
    Enjoy Life Without Financial Stress

CHAPTER 3 ... 47
Prioritize Vitality - Live a Vibrant Life
    Healthcare
    Medicare
    Maintain Physical Health
    Exercise and Living
    Diet and Living
    Mental Health and Living

CHAPTER 4   65
Own Your Identity - Build Resilience and Confidence
- What is Identity?
- Our Changing Self-Identity
- Self-Confidence
- Resilience Matters

CHAPTER 5   79
Woven Bonds - Build and Maintain Relationships
- Community
- Social Connections
- Consciously Creating Connections
- Route #1 The DIY Method
- Route #2 The Ready-made Method
- Making the Choice
- The Ties That Bind
- Dating
- An Easy Way You Can Help Someone Else

CHAPTER 6   97
Energize Your Essence - Discover New Passions
- Avocation
- Lifelong Learning
- Overcoming Fear of the Unknown
- Stuff Gets in the Way
- Support

CHAPTER 7   109
Renew Yourself - Create a Joyful Environment
- Living Space
- Mind Space

Spirit Space

CHAPTER 8   121

The Path to Serenity

    Embracing Change

    Embracing Relationships

    Embracing Simplicity

    Embracing the Future

CONCLUSION   131

References   133

INTRODUCTION

Some of us may be slightly surprised to be looking at the future from a solo perspective. We are by no means alone. Nearly half of U.S. adults are single, including people who are divorced, widowed, and never married, according to September 2023 data from the American Community Survey. In 2020, over a quarter of U.S. households were comprised of one person.

Our lives unfold uniquely, shaped by various circumstances. Here are some common paths that may lead to our singleness:

Personal Choice: Some individuals actively choose a solo lifestyle, deciding to embrace independence and solitude. This choice may be influenced by a desire for self-discovery, personal growth, or a preference for autonomy.

Divorce or Separation: The end of a marriage or a long-term relationship can lead to a solo status in later years. Individuals may find themselves navigating life independently following a divorce or separation, adjusting to a new chapter without a partner.

Widowhood: The loss of a spouse through death is a significant life event that can result in a solo status. Widows face the challenges and opportunities of aging alone.

Childlessness: For those without children or close family members, the aging journey may be experienced without the traditional support system that family often provides. This circumstance can lead to a more independent lifestyle but also may create a solo status.

Geographic Mobility: Frequent relocations or living in a different location from existing family can contribute to a solo status, particularly if one's social connections are not maintained across moves. Geographic mobility results in a more transient and independent lifestyle.

Relationship Changes: Shifts in friendships or changes in social circles can impact our support network. Individuals who experience significant changes in their relationships may find themselves adapting to a solo status as they age.

Career-Focused Lifestyle: A career-focused lifestyle that involves extensive travel, long working hours, or a commitment to professional pursuits may lead to a more independent and solo lifestyle. The demands of a career can influence personal relationships.

Loss of Family and Friends: The passing of close family members and friends over the years can contribute to a solo status. As our social circle becomes smaller, we may face the challenges of aging without our familiar support network.

Personal circumstances, choices, or a combination of factors can contribute to a solo status. These may also include health considerations or any number of other unique life experiences. Our lives unfold based on the choices we make and the resilience we cultivate in life.

The complexities of aging take on a unique perspective for those of us who find we are doing it alone. Within the pages of this book, we will refer to our unique status as "Soloists," and going forward, we will capitalize the "S." We will extend this naming convention to two-word phrases like "Solo Women" and "Solo Lifestyle," etc. We want to designate these terms as a reference to our dignity and resilience. In musical performances, Soloists noticeably carry the responsibility of a successful performance. Similar to a solo musical performance, Soloists in life carry the weight of their own performance.

Even though our title words are "AGING SOLO", we will focus on living instead of aging. By emphasizing living, we celebrate our past experiences, prioritize present-moment awareness, and look ahead to growth and discovery. Rather than seeing aging as a limitation or decline, focusing on living empowers us to cultivate vitality and engage fully in the joys and challenges of life ahead. It reminds us that age is not a barrier to living fully. It is an incentive to embrace all that life offers with enthusiasm.

According to SARA ZEFF GEBER, in her blog called Generations for the American Society on Aging, "Thanks to the pandemic, isolation and loneliness are now front and center in new research on the pitfalls of aging. The media has picked up on the trend as well and along with this came a much greater awareness of Solo Aging. What had been obscure and rarely discussed in 2019 was a hot topic... People were finally paying attention to a demographic phenomenon that will, in my opinion, be a significant challenge to individuals and society as the boomers move into their later years."

With these thoughts in mind, we will consider an
E.M.P.O.W.E.R. Path
toward living with grace and joy. We will address some of the unique challenges and opportunities of Solo Living. Each letter in **E.M.P.O.W.E.R.** is a stepping stone toward a future filled with confidence and purpose.

E. Embrace the Challenge - Living Solo: We acknowledge our unique circumstances, face them head-on, and turn them into opportunities for personal growth.

M. Manage Money Mindfully - Welcome Desires: Our financial security is the cornerstone of a worry-free life. This section provides practical advice and a mindful approach to managing finances, ensuring a stable future.

P. Prioritize Vitality - Live a Vibrant Life: This section goes into the holistic well-being of Solo Women—physically, mentally, and emotionally. It's a guide to maintaining vitality and embracing life ahead with energy and enthusiasm.

O. Own Your Identity - Build Resilience and Confidence: Solo Women have unique stories to tell, and this section encourages us to recognize own our identity, build resilience, and exude confidence as we navigate the next phase of life.

W. Woven Bonds - Build and Maintain Relationships: While the journey may be Solo, it's not lacking connections. This part explores the importance of meaningful relationships, how to build them, and their value in a Solo Life.

E. Energize Your Essence - Discovering New Passions: Life is an ongoing discovery, and this chapter encourages the exploration of new passions and hobbies. It's about infusing life with purpose and excitement.

R. Renew Yourself - Create a Joyful Environment: The final stepping stone explains the importance of consciously creating a joyful environment. Our future is built by curating our best life.

The resulting **Path** leads us to peace of mind—a life of grace, joy, and dignity. We find peace within ourselves and realize that the wisdom that comes with the passage of time is within our reach.

This book is tailored specifically for Solo Women, acknowledging our unique circumstances and opening a future that radiates confidence and fulfillment. The **E.M.P.O.W.E.R. Path** will provide the transformative process. We are Soloists, creating a confident future.

At the end of each chapter, you'll find Tailored Solutions created to address the theme that we discussed. While some strategies appear similar, they offer a slightly different perspective on each issue.

These strategies often have overlapping benefits and applications, offering versatility and flexibility. Some solutions may address more than one point, providing you with a range of options for life's complexities. Feel free to explore and identify the strategies that resonate with your unique situation. We aim to give readers the tools they need to navigate Solo Living successfully.

CHAPTER 1

EMBRACE THE CHALLENGE - LIVING SOLO

The first "E" on the E.M.P.O.W.E.R Path stands for Embrace the Challenge.

Living Solo, or embracing the role of a Soloist, opens up a world of unique challenges and opportunities. We begin walking the path, recognizing that our most significant obstacles often stem from our own perceptions. Shifting our perspective unlocks the door to better possibilities and a promising future. We all want an inviting and engaging future. Our primary goal must be to acknowledge what we see as a challenge and transform it into an opportunity.

There is a huge transformative power in examining our deepest fears associated with Solo Living. Fear is a natural and pervasive emotion; understanding these fears is the first step towards harnessing their power. We don't need to let our fears control us. We want to shift from a perception that sees living alone as a limitation to one that empowers us.

What Are We Afraid of?

Let's look at what some of our fears might be. Keep in mind that all of us may not be burdened with every single one of these. If not, you've got a head start! The list below represents 7 of the top fears we, as Soloist Women, deal with.

Fear of Being Judged as a Failure: Some people carry the unspoken burden of fearing judgment from others, worried they'll be seen as a failure for being alone at this point in life. Or worse, being invisible – not being seen at all. This fear is deeply rooted in societal expectations. It often leads to a sense of inadequacy and shame about living alone.

Dread of Loneliness: Is there a secret terror of facing the years ahead engulfed in loneliness? The silent house, the absence of daily conversations, and the fear of being forgotten or overlooked by society are daunting prospects.

Anxieties about Health and Dependence: There's a deep, often unvoiced fear about health and our mental capacities deteriorating with age. The thought of losing independence and relying on others for basic care is scary and strikes our sense of dignity.

Dealing with Grief and Emotional Scars: Often, we carry hidden grief from past losses and unresolved emotional pain. The fear of facing these sorrows alone, without support, adds an invisible weight to everyday life.

Grappling with the Fear of Death: We may carry a burden that is rooted in the apprehension and anxiety about the inevitability of death. This fear extends beyond the natural concern for mortality and confronts us with questions about the unknown aspects of what comes after life. It often manifests as a deep-seated fear of the unknown, the loss of control, and the cessation of one's existence. This fear can be intertwined with cultural, religious, and personal beliefs about the afterlife. It can be worsened by societal reluctance to openly discuss death, creating a sense of taboo around the subject. The fear of dying may lead us to grapple with questions of meaning, legacy, and the impact we will leave on the world.

Apprehension About Fading Beauty: The fear of losing our good looks is rooted in cultural norms prioritizing youthfulness. It can result in pressure to maintain a certain standard of beauty, leading to anxieties about self-worth and acceptance. We may become very concerned about wrinkles, changes in body shape, and the emphasis on an idealized image of beauty that aligns differently from the natural aging process.

Fears of Financial Ruin: There may be private anxieties about financial stability. The prospect of outliving our savings or facing choices between essentials like medication and food may be a source of sleepless nights and unspoken worries.

This is by no means the entire list of fears that our minds can come up with. These fears represent complex emotions that may affect us to varying degrees. In this chapter, we will look deeper into those listed above.

This discussion on fears associated with Solo Living and other challenges is intended for informational and reflective purposes. It is crucial to recognize that these fears may go beyond the level of ordinary concerns and, in some cases, may require professional help.

If you find that these fears are significantly affecting your mental health, causing distress, or leading to an overwhelming sense of anxiety, we strongly advise you to seek guidance from qualified professionals. These health professionals, counselors, and therapists are trained to provide personalized support and strategies to deal with complex emotions. Getting support is a sign of strength, and professional help can be instrumental in navigating life's challenges.

Our intent here is to discover that we can replace each of these fears with a positive operational framework. The way to do that is by making space in our thoughts for alternative ideas. First, we will examine how true each fear statement is in relation to reality. When we shed light on them and really examine each one, they become less threatening. We find that we can come up with better feeling thoughts on each issue.

Just the Facts, Ma'am!

Does society really judge the aging single woman? Here are some facts and perspectives that challenge the fear of any judgment associated with living alone:

Fact - Changing Demographics worldwide show a significant increase in the number of people living alone, indicating a shift in societal norms. The Solo status is becoming increasingly common, highlighting that it's not an unusual or stigmatized circumstance but rather a reflection of evolving societal structures.

Fact - Many individuals who are alone actively choose this lifestyle. The decision to remain alone is often a conscious choice, challenging the assumption that it results from rejection or failure.

Fact - Soloists can maintain robust social connections and support networks in many ways through friends, family, and community involvement. The quality of relationships and support systems can counter feelings of inadequacy, emphasizing that living alone does not mean being entirely isolated or unsupported.

Fact - Many accomplished individuals, including artists, scientists, and entrepreneurs, have led fulfilling lives while living Solo.

Fact - Being alone can provide opportunities for self-discovery, personal growth, and the cultivation of independence. Emphasizing the positive aspects of autonomy and self-reliance challenges the idea that aging alone is inherently negative or indicative of failure.

Fact - Research suggests that the impact of living alone on well-being and mental health varies widely, and many individuals living alone report high levels of life satisfaction. Focusing on mental and emotional well-being helps debunk the assumption that it universally leads to inadequacy and shame.

A positive perspective would be redefining our Solo status as an opportunity for personal growth and self-discovery. We can recognize the uniqueness of our lives and realize that society's expectations are not absolute benchmarks. We can challenge the conventional definition of how our lives should look and live with authentic and fulfilling experiences in the future.

How can we stop the dread of loneliness? As we live longer, this can be a common concern, but there are several facts and perspectives that provide reassurance and challenge this fear:

Fact - With advancing technology, Soloists have more opportunities than ever to stay socially connected. Social media, video calls, and online communities can help combat loneliness because location does not prevent us from communicating and connecting with friends and family, wherever they may be.

Fact - Many local communities offer programs specifically designed to engage older individuals in social activities. Participating in community events, clubs, or volunteering can create social connections and alleviate the fear of loneliness.

Fact - Family structures are diverse, and many Soloists are part of extended family networks. Even if family members don't live nearby, family ties can still be maintained. Support from extended family members, such as grandchildren or siblings, can provide a strong sense of belonging and reduce feelings of loneliness.

Fact - There's a growing acknowledgment of the importance of addressing social isolation. As society becomes increasingly aware of the detrimental effects of social isolation, efforts to combat this issue are gaining momentum. Communities are implementing innovative solutions to specifically create connection and support because they recognize the impact of social interaction on overall well-being.

Fact - Participating in health and wellness programs can contribute to both physical and social well-being. Activities like group exercise classes or wellness workshops promote health and create opportunities for social interaction, reducing the likelihood of loneliness.

Fact - Housing options tailored for Soloists often incorporate communal spaces and social activities. Choosing living arrangements that encourage social interaction within the community reduces the fear of loneliness and promotes a sense of belonging.

Fact - Pets can be excellent companions and provide emotional support. Mental health professionals agree that having a pet can reduce feelings of isolation and contribute to personal well-being.

Fact - Practices like mindfulness and mental health initiatives contribute to emotional resilience. Prioritizing mental well-being enhances our ability to cope with the fear of loneliness and promotes a positive outlook on life.

These facts and perspectives underscore the many opportunities available to address the dread of loneliness, emphasizing the potential for meaningful connections, social engagement, and a fulfilling life. From a positive perspective, the dread of loneliness can be transformed into an opportunity to cultivate rich and meaningful social connections. Embrace the challenge by actively concentrating on friendships and participating in activities of interest. The fear of loneliness becomes an incentive for building our own supportive network. Doing that gives us a future filled with shared experiences and a sense of belonging. Seeing loneliness as a call to deepen social connections transforms it into a powerful force for creating a vibrant and fulfilling social life.

How can we address hypochondriasis (health anxiety)? Anxieties about health and dependence as we live longer are common. Still, there are several facts and perspectives that can provide reassurance and challenge these fears:

Fact - The average 60-year-old today has a 4.8% chance of developing Alzheimer's disease in their life; that's a 95.2% chance you won't!

Fact - Medical advancements have significantly improved the prevention and treatment of various health conditions. Access to medical technologies and treatments increases the potential for maintaining good health and managing health concerns effectively.

Fact - Being proactive about healthcare, which involves regular check-ups, screenings, and maintaining a healthy lifestyle, helps prevent many health issues from escalating into severe problems.

Fact - Life expectancy has generally increased, indicating overall improvements in health and living conditions. Longer life expectancy suggests that many individuals are enjoying healthier and more active lives in their later years.

Fact - Technology has led to the development of various assistive devices to enhance independence. From mobility aids to smart home technologies, these innovations empower us to maintain a higher level of independence despite potential health challenges.

Fact - Planning for long-term care is more accessible than ever. Adequate financial planning, including insurance and retirement savings, can provide a safety net and alleviate concerns about potential healthcare costs.

Fact - Access to health information and education is widespread. Understanding our current health, making informed decisions, and actively participating in healthcare decisions empower us to take control of our well-being.

Fact - Positive aging narratives and role models challenge stereotypes of decline in old age. Stories of individuals leading active and fulfilling lives counter negative perceptions, supporting a more optimistic view of aging.

Focusing on this evidence reduces anxieties about health and dependence. These facts support positive ways to think about our health and independence. Reducing anxieties about health and dependence involves a shift towards prioritizing holistic well-being. Instead of viewing health concerns as insurmountable obstacles, we can approach them as opportunities to enhance our overall wellness. We can answer the challenge by adopting healthy lifestyle choices, exercising regularly, and focusing on mental well-being. By proactively addressing health concerns, we empower ourselves.

How can we fight the battle with grief and emotional scars that we have accumulated over a lifetime? Facing grief and emotional scars is a profound challenge at any stage of life, but there are some facts and perspectives that can provide comfort and challenge this fear:

Fact - Human beings exhibit remarkable resilience across their lifespan. Research indicates that individuals adapt and recover from grief if they are willing to work with it. This can be very difficult internal work, but we have the capacity to find new sources of joy and meaning even after experiencing significant losses.

Fact - Mental health support services and awareness have increased. Access to counseling, therapy, and support groups provides valuable assistance for addressing grief and emotional scars, helping us get through these challenges with professional guidance.

Fact - Over our lifetime, we have developed coping strategies and emotional resilience that we can rely on. We bring with us a wealth of life experiences. With them, we have developed coping mechanisms, enabling us to draw on our inner strength to confront and manage emotional scars.

Fact - Expressive arts and therapeutic interventions can help in emotional healing. Engaging in creative outlets like art, music, or writing, as well as therapeutic interventions, can provide ways to process emotions associated with grief and anxiety. Fortunately, as most of us are retirees, we have the time to do these activities.

Fact - Humans are naturally inclined to find meaning in their life stories. Engaging in life review processes and finding meaning in our experiences, both positive and negative, contributes to a sense of closure and purpose.

Fact - Many other women have shared their stories of personal growth through adversity. These narratives of overcoming grief and emotional scars show us the way through our own pain. Their stories underscore the potential for transformative growth, showing us, by their example, that our challenges can also be overcome.

Fact - Sharing our experiences and advice with others can be a source of fulfillment and a way to contribute positively to the lives of others, giving us a sense of purpose.

These facts and perspectives emphasize the potential for healing, growth, and resilience in the face of grief and emotional scars, offering hope and a more positive outlook on our emotional challenges.

A positive perspective in this area would be to embrace the depth of our emotions and seek support from friends in conversation or through therapy, counseling, or other support groups. Embracing the scars of our past as part of our unique narrative empowers us to face future challenges with newfound strength and compassion.

How do the majority of people handle the fear of dying? The truth is that everything that is alive will die, including plants, animals, and people. Finding a way to deal with this knowledge is an essential step in living longer. Handling the fear of dying is a deeply personal and subjective experience, and we may approach it in various ways based on our beliefs, values, and coping mechanisms. If you have been putting off developing a personal framework for death, it may be an excellent time to create whatever will work best for you. We suggest checking out a YouTube channel called Exit Plan which was developed by Diana Mikas.

Fact - Many people find solace and comfort in their spiritual or religious beliefs. Faith can provide a framework for understanding the meaning of life, death, and the existence beyond, helping to alleviate the fear of dying by offering a sense of purpose and connection.

Fact - Some of us cope with the fear of dying through philosophical reflection. Engaging in contemplation about the nature of life and death, existentialism, or philosophical perspectives on mortality can provide a framework for acceptance and understanding.

Fact - Building and maintaining strong relationships with family, friends, and loved ones can be a powerful way to handle the fear of dying. Meaningful connections contribute to a sense of belonging and support, offering emotional reassurance during challenging times.

Fact - Whether through personal achievements, contributions to society, or leaving a positive impact on others, creating a legacy can be a way to handle the fear of dying. It provides a sense of continuity beyond one's own existence.

Fact - Seek knowledge and understanding. Some people alleviate the fear of dying by seeking knowledge about what happens physically during the dying process. Understanding death as a natural part of life can contribute to a more accepting mindset.

Fact - Taking practical steps, such as engaging in end-of-life planning, can help individuals gain a sense of control and preparedness. This may involve discussing healthcare preferences and making final arrangements like specific funeral details.

Fact - Seeking the assistance of mental health professionals, such as therapists or counselors, can provide a safe space to explore and address fears of dying. Therapeutic interventions may include cognitive-behavioral techniques, mindfulness, or existential therapy.

Fact - Embracing mindfulness and living in the present moment can help us focus on the joys and experiences of life rather than dwelling excessively on the fear of dying. Mindfulness practices promote a sense of peace and acceptance.

These facts and perspectives show us various tools and strategies that have worked for others, possibly since the beginning of time. It's important to note that all or any combination of these approaches might be helpful. Alternatively, we are free to adopt other personalized strategies based on our unique circumstances. The fear of dying is a complex and individualized aspect of the human experience, and finding ways to navigate it may involve a combination of personal reflection and emotional support.

As we take the time to develop a positive perspective in this area, consider this: From the dawn of human history, our species has dealt with the mysteries surrounding the beginning and the end of life. Our evolving understanding of science, medicine, and psychology continues to shape how we approach the end of life. Humanity has always been on a quest to find meaning in life and death, transcend fear, and embrace the profound mystery of our existence. In this human experience, we participate in a shared endeavor to reconcile the finite nature of life with the infinite possibilities of the human spirit.

What can women do to address the fear of losing their beauty?

Despite society's emphasis on physical beauty, we must acknowledge and value the many different qualities in others and ourselves. These qualities extend beyond external appearances. Isn't this an idea we have tried to instill in our young people? Beauty goes beyond what we see. We have many abilities and talents. We possess a diverse range of skills that contribute significantly to our identity. Physical appearance is just one aspect of a person's overall makeup, and highlighting other qualities showcases the richness of our being. Here are some facts that challenge the notion that physical beauty is so important:

Fact - Intelligence, creativity, and intellectual capabilities are attractive aspects. Emphasizing these qualities underscores the importance of mental and cognitive abilities.

Fact - Qualities such as kindness, empathy, and compassion are integral to building meaningful social connections. These traits contribute to the well-being of everyone we come into contact with. These qualities affect our communities and emphasize the significance of inner character.

Fact - Personal achievements and contributions to society, often have a lasting and meaningful effect on others. These accomplishments go beyond physical appearance, demonstrating the value of our actions and influence.

Fact - Resilience and adaptability in the face of adversity are qualities that highlight our strength and character. The ability to work through problems, learn from experiences, and grow as a person underscores the importance of inner resilience.

Fact - Emotional intelligence, including self-awareness, self-regulation, and empathy, play an important role in personal relationships and overall well-being. These aspects contribute significantly to the quality of interactions, transcending physical beauty.

Fact - Courage and integrity shape ethical decision-making and contribute to moral character. Demonstrating these qualities reflects a commitment to principles that extend beyond external appearances.

Fact - Effective interpersonal skills and communication that we have built over a lifetime help us create positive relationships and collaborations. These skills are key to success in our personal and professional lives, emphasizing the importance of effective communication over physical appearance.

Fact - A sense of humor, joy, and the ability to bring positivity into our own lives and the lives of others contribute to emotional well-being. These aspects of personality play a more significant role in overall happiness than physical appearance alone.

Fact - Accumulated life wisdom and experiences shape our perspective and understanding of the world. The depth of knowledge gained over time often surpasses the superficial emphasis on physical beauty, highlighting the importance of inner growth.

These facts emphasize that physical beauty is just one aspect of a person's identity, and numerous other qualities contribute to our worth.

Recognizing and valuing the range of our attributes proves our personal value and significance. Emphasizing accomplishment over beauty creates a more inclusive and empowering society. It highlights the inherent worth of every individual, emphasizing their meaningful contributions and accomplishments rather than superficial attributes like physical appearance.

How can we overcome those fears of financial destitution? Addressing concerns of financial destitution involves considering various factors that can provide reassurance. Here are some facts and perspectives:

Fact - Various retirement savings options are available during our working years. Contributing to retirement accounts, such as 401(k)s or IRAs, allows us to build a financial cushion for later on, helping reduce the fear of poverty.

Fact - Social Security provides a safety net for eligible individuals in retirement. Understanding and maximizing Social Security benefits can contribute to a more stable financial situation, providing a guaranteed source of income for retirees.

Fact - Financial planning services are there to help us plan for retirement. Seeking professional financial advice and creating a comprehensive financial plan can address concerns and provide a roadmap for achieving financial security.

Fact - Various government assistance programs exist to support Soloists in need. Programs like Medicaid, Supplemental Security Income (SSI), and other state-specific initiatives can assist those facing financial challenges with healthcare and living expenses.

Fact - Diversifying investments can help protect against financial volatility. Investing in a diversified portfolio, including stocks, bonds, and other assets, can yield returns that contribute to long-term financial stability.

Fact - Many Solo Women continue to work or explore part-time employment options. Engaging in part-time work or consulting opportunities can supplement income in retirement, offering us a sense of financial security.

Fact - Some retirement income sources, like Social Security, may include cost-of-living adjustments. These Cost-of-Living Adjustment programs, or COLAs, can help retirees keep pace with inflation, maintaining the purchasing power of their income over time.

Fact - Long-term care insurance can help cover healthcare costs associated with aging. Planning for potential long-term care needs through insurance can prevent financial strain and protect assets in the event of health challenges.

Fact - Adjusting lifestyle and spending habits can contribute to financial stability. Being mindful of budgeting, reducing unnecessary expenses, and making informed financial decisions can help us live within our means in retirement.

These facts and perspectives emphasize the various tools and strategies available to address financial concerns, promoting a more secure and confident approach to our later years.

Turn the fears of financial ruin into an opportunity for strategic financial empowerment. Answer the challenge by taking a proactive approach to financial planning, seeking professional advice, and exploring diverse income streams. Instead of viewing financial fears as threats, transform them into motivators for informed decision-making and long-term stability. Embracing the financial planning challenge ensures that Living Solo becomes reinforced by financial resilience and security.

As we work through the challenges presented by these fears and gain confidence in transforming fears into opportunities, remember that empowerment lies in addressing the challenges and facing them with authenticity and grace. Our journey through life is a mosaic of experiences. We shape a narrative of growth, resilience, and enduring empowerment by embracing the challenges. In our individual stories of living, the challenges mentioned may not be the only ones we face. But by taking the example of those discussed here, we gain knowledge and strength to face any additional challenges that may come our way.

Retirement

Retirement marks the beginning of an exciting new segment of life filled with possibilities and opportunities for personal growth and fulfillment. We can truly claim retirement as our domain. It's a time to rediscover passions, explore new things, and savor the freedom to pursue interests without the constraints of a busy career. With more time to spend with loved ones, travel to new destinations, and immerse ourselves in leisure activities, retirement offers the chance to truly embrace the joys of living and create cherished memories that will last a lifetime. It's a time to celebrate all that has been accomplished and to look forward to the adventures yet to come. Retirement is a golden opportunity to live life fully and make every moment count!

Reaching retirement or even thinking about retirement, we naturally contemplate the financial landscape ahead. The good news is that we have many financial tools and strategies at our disposal. From accessing savings accumulated during our working years to exploring the possibilities offered by Social Security and other government assistance programs, we can get some idea about the foundation of our financial security.

As we proceed to the next chapter, we will go deeper into our finances by looking at money management. Our goal will be to align our resources with our values and aspirations. Even though we may have avoided all thoughts of money matters in the past, we will begin the next chapter with an invitation to leave fear behind and engage in a thoughtful and purposeful relationship with our finances. Many of us may resist looking at our financial situation, but taking a good look at it is essential. Facing reality and adjusting to it removes the uncertainty that may be causing our fears.

***

THE TAILORED SOLUTIONS

Arm yourself with the facts. It's evident that many of the fears surrounding growing older as a Soloist are rooted in misconceptions rather than reality.

Maintain an optimistic outlook. Challenge the notion of societal judgment by recognizing the evolving demographics of Solo Living.

Develop a philosophy that supports your thoughts about life and death.

Ask for help when you need it. Take advantage of professional support for any issue that you feel is overwhelming your ability to enjoy life fully.

Look for the lessons you can learn. Focus on the positive aspects of autonomy and self-reliance that come with Solo Living.

CHAPTER 2

MANAGE MONEY MINDFULLY - WELCOME DESIRES

The letter "M" on the E.M.P.O.W.E.R Path stands for Manage Money Mindfully

Emotional and logistical factors can contribute to some Soloists' resistance to tending to details like health insurance and end-of-life legal issues. Many of us may procrastinate and avoid these subjects as long as possible. In some cases, until it's too late. We may resist tending to these details for several reasons. We may consider them unpleasant topics. We may find them difficult or too complex. We may not understand how important they are. Or we fear change.

This chapter will address these issues as simply and nonthreateningly as possible. In fact, we will present the "bare bones" only. We encourage you to look into all aspects of these topics further if you want more information. But, if you're the type of person who hears the words "finance" or "legal" in any form and glazes over, we'll try to make this chapter as painless as possible for you. Here's one more fact: focusing on getting these high-priority items in place will make your life much smoother. The best way to take worry out of your future is to address it head-on.

With that in mind, we will enthusiastically move into this chapter, fueled by optimism. Get ready to empower yourself with the knowledge that managing money mindfully is a practical necessity and a superpower. As we get into the balancing act of dollars and dreams, recognize that every dollar has the potential to move you closer to your aspirations. The future holds possibilities, and the background music has the melody of competent money management. You have the power to shape your financial future.

Smart money management will create a *nearly* stress-free life. We will concentrate on providing practical advice on managing finances, budgeting, and retirement planning. We will also discuss strategies for achieving financial independence and living comfortably within our means.

Our goal is to empower Soloists to thrive in a state of financial independence, where our lifestyle comes from a place of confidence. Solid financial knowledge gives us the structure to make choices that align with personal values and aspirations. We can then deal with the complexities of living within our means. Complete knowledge about our finances will determine our choices in housing, emergency preparedness, and legacy considerations.

Financial Planning

Addressing financial empowerment is a bold move towards securing your future and achieving your goals. While the prospect of managing finances may seem daunting, rest assured that you have the power to take control and create a bright financial future for yourself. From organizing and understanding your financial landscape to safeguarding your credit and creating a realistic budget, each step is crucial for your financial well-being. With determination and a commitment to taking action, you can make your way through the complexities of personal finance and emerge stronger than before.

In general, there are 4 steps to getting a handle on finances:

Step 1: Get organized and gather key financial documents.

Step 2: Understand what you own and what you owe.

Step 3: Know how much your bills are and the dates that they are due.

Step 4: Create your budget.

It's important to keep all of this paperwork in one place. You can get started on steps 1 through 3 as soon as possible. Budgeting is an ongoing process. Start by making a high-level list of where you think your expenses are, and be ready to make adjustments to your budget frequently. There is a lot of power in accomplishing the steps and writing the information down on paper. All the uncertainty suddenly disappears as soon as it's organized. Now, you know! Now you can begin working with this information to plan your future.

If you don't feel confident about any of these steps, you can find help from various resources.

Online Resources: One site that seems very user-friendly is called Principal. On this site, you can download a PDF file to get you started. You can customize their worksheets and label them according to the steps above: What I Own & What I Owe, My Current Bills, and My Budget. Take advantage of other online resources by searching for financial planning websites, budgeting tools, and educational videos to learn more about managing your finances effectively.

Financial Literacy Workshops: Many community organizations, libraries, and financial institutions offer workshops and seminars on basic financial literacy topics, including budgeting, debt management, and financial planning.

Financial Advisors: Consider looking for guidance from a certified financial advisor who can provide personalized advice and assistance tailored to your specific financial situation and goals.

Credit Counseling Services: Nonprofit credit counseling agencies offer free or low-cost services to help individuals manage debt, improve credit scores, and develop strategies for financial stability.

Government Resources: Explore government websites and programs that offer information and assistance on financial topics, such as the Consumer Financial Protection Bureau (CFPB) or the Department of Housing and Urban Development (HUD).

Peer Support Groups: Joining a support group or community forum focused on personal finance can provide valuable insights, tips, and encouragement from others facing similar challenges.

Books and Publications: There are many books, magazines, and online articles available that cover a wide range of financial topics, from basic money management to advanced investment strategies.

Budgeting Apps: Utilize budgeting apps and tools that can help you track your expenses, set financial goals, and manage your budget more effectively.

Local Assistance Programs: Some communities offer assistance programs or resources for individuals struggling with financial issues, such as utility bill assistance or financial counseling services.

Family and Friends: Don't hesitate to reach out to trusted family members or friends who may be able to offer support, advice, or referrals to helpful resources.

Dealing with finances can be particularly challenging when we're unexpectedly thrust into facing them for the first time. This situation can be especially tricky if we don't have prior experience managing financial matters. Your situation could be the result of the sudden death of a partner or because of a divorce. But rest assured that you are fully capable of handling your finances, and help is available if you need it.

The divorce rate for those over age 50 has doubled in the past 20 years, according to research by Divorce.com. So, for those in their 40s, 50s, and beyond, this is a real planning concern. There are 3 resources that may help specifically for a divorce situation. They are the IDFA (Institute for Divorce Financial Analysts), the ADFP (Association of Divorce Financial Planners), and a CDFA (Certified Divorce Financial Analyst).

Remember, it's okay to seek help when you need it, and taking proactive steps to improve your financial skills is a valuable investment in your future.

This is a snapshot in the life of Carol Tucker, described in an article found on a website called FORTUNE WELL:

> Carol Tucker, 63, is a lab manager at a medical school in Atlanta, Georgia, and has been divorced for about five years after a 27-year marriage. She says being single can be challenging regarding insurance and thinking about the future, "Who will care for me if I'm unable to care for myself?"
>
> Carol did her research and turned to friends to learn their strategies for dealing with the fallout from divorce. She says being single has made her agile in preparing for aging and the future. She's "ready to pivot," as she calls it. As a result, she's modified her will and invested more of her income in her long-term disability insurance, and each year, she reassesses her plans and financials. When seeking mental and financial support as a single woman, Carol says she turns to her trusted circle that she calls her "Cabinet."
>
> "I'm quite fortunate to have a wonderful network from extended family, friends, and church community."

We'll follow Carol Tucker through some of her steps to gain her financial agility.

First, let's look at what some of her initial challenges might have been:

Financial Adjustments: Divorce often involves financial changes. Adapting to a new budget, managing assets, and understanding the financial implications of the divorce settlement can be challenging. This includes issues related to property division, alimony, and retirement accounts.

Emotional Adjustment: Coping with the emotional aftermath of a divorce can be significant. Feelings of loss, grief, and uncertainty about the future may arise, requiring emotional resilience on our part and support from friends, family, and/or counseling.

Social Networks and Relationships: Divorce can impact social networks. A newly divorced woman may need to navigate changes in friendships, family dynamics, and social connections. It may require rebuilding a supportive network.

Housing and Living Arrangements: Deciding on living arrangements and potentially relocating can be a huge challenge. It involves considering housing options, like downsizing, staying in the family home, or exploring new living arrangements.

Legal and Administrative Processes: Navigating legal processes related to divorce, such as finalizing paperwork, updating legal documents, and understanding post-divorce rights and responsibilities, can be complex. Seeking legal guidance is essential during this phase.

Healthcare and Insurance Considerations: Assessing healthcare coverage and insurance needs to be done. Understanding changes in health insurance, evaluating long-term care options, and ensuring access to necessary healthcare services are important aspects of post-divorce life.

Identity and Self-Rediscovery: Divorce can prompt a reevaluation of identity and self-discovery. Rediscovering personal interests, goals, and aspirations is a part of the healing and rebuilding process.

Future Planning and Retirement: A newly single woman may need to reassess her future plans and retirement goals. Understanding the impact of a new state of being regarding retirement savings, revisiting financial goals, and planning for the next chapter of life become essential considerations.

This list is overwhelming. Anyone who has experienced any part of this list and come through it successfully, as Carol seems to have done is to be applauded. Navigating these initial challenges requires resilience, support, and careful planning.

In Carol's case, she was hit with the full list all at once because of her particular divorce situation. But all of us must deal with our finances at some point. Wise Soloists may have had the option of long-term planning that sudden divorcees and widows may not have.

Preparing for our financial future involves establishing a solid foundation for economic stability and long-term well-being. We've categorized three priorities based on urgency because some issues require immediate attention while others can be addressed later. If you've unexpectedly found yourself single, it's essential to handle these matters as soon as you're emotionally ready. Here are the bare bones of what we need:

TOP PRIORITY

Financial Literacy: Become informed about any and all personal income. You need to know where all available money comes from and how to access it. If you don't know where you stand, you are financially helpless. You need to verify and document all income sources. Once you have this information, you can develop strategies and make informed financial decisions based on a solid understanding of what is available to you.

If you have not been thrust into an emergency situation and know this moment is on its way, you can begin more leisurely. The sooner you start planning for your financial future, the better. The same advice holds true if you feel you won't be relying on retirement income for 20 or more years. You absolutely need to know what your income is now and will be in the future.

Debt Management: Developing a strategy for managing and reducing existing debts is crucial. Debt gathers interest, which means it is costing you money. If possible, try to avoid carrying debt altogether. If it's not possible, remember that it's a very good idea to eliminate it as soon as possible. Prioritize high-interest debts to pay those off quickly. Explore repayment options to lift these financial burdens. Make it a personal goal to keep debt as low as possible.

Budgeting: Now is the time to create a detailed budget that outlines income, expenses, and savings goals. Track spending habits to identify areas for potential savings. You want to make sure that your money is being spent wisely. Your financial landscape will change over time. Any time it changes, your budget needs to be reevaluated and tweaked to reflect your current situation.

Regular Financial Checkups: During the first week of each month, find a point to take a small amount of time and check in on how things are going in your financial life. Look at what happened last month. Does anything need to be updated or changed in some way? Check up on your finances to ensure you're progressing toward your goals. This is when you adjust your budget again and make decisions about any changes. You owe it to yourself to keep watch. Regular monitoring ensures that your financial plans still align with your changing life.

Deal with Emergencies: Don't be caught off guard. Emergencies happen, and we should do our best to be prepared. Dealing with an emergency is less stressful if you already know where you stand financially. Need car repairs or a major appliance? By keeping a close eye on your finances, you'll see if you can respond to a current emergency easily by using savings or if now is the time that you must increase your credit debt because there's no other way to pay for what has happened. If you find yourself needing to use credit for an emergency, you can take comfort in knowing that you've been managing repayments successfully for some time. So, this new debt shouldn't unnecessarily add stress to your personal life. You are totally capable of handling your finances.

Living Below Means: Cultivate a lifestyle that allows for living below your means. Everyone wants to be comfortable with their present financial circumstances. Less stress and more ease is a lovely way to live. If you're not experiencing that now, devise a plan to create it. Whether you're thrown suddenly into the financial caretaker role, or you've seen it coming for years, living below or at your means is possible. If you need help getting there, more assistance is available than you would think. Here are some suggestions:

- Contact a certified financial counselor or financial planner if you want in-person help. Nonprofit organizations, community centers, or financial institutions may offer free or low-cost counseling services.

- Search online for debt consolidation, budgeting tools, and apps or platforms like Reddit's personal finance subreddit or community websites which may provide valuable insights and support.

- If printed material is better for you, look for books by authors like Dave Ramsey, Suze Orman, and Elizabeth Warren. They have written extensively on budgeting and financial discipline.

- There are also educational courses, peer support groups, and employee assistance programs that you can investigate.

These options are relatively user-friendly and can be pursued independently. Whatever you do, don't do nothing! You have a future to care about, and you want it to be enjoyable.

SECONDARY LIST

We list this group second, but not because it's less important. These things can wait until the top-priority items are taken care of. These things may require some research or some time to set up. But they still need to be done.

Insurance Coverage: Look into adequate insurance coverage, including health, life, home, and auto insurance. Regularly review insurance policies to ensure coverage matches your current needs and circumstances. If there are in-force policies, they may need to be updated according to your current life circumstances. In some cases, coverage can be reduced if you are now a household of one or only need to insure one car.

Retirement Savings: Contribute regularly to retirement savings accounts, such as 401(k)s or IRAs, if you are still working. Adjust amounts according to your budget. Take advantage of employer-sponsored retirement plans and explore additional investment options for long-term financial security.

Investing Basics: Understand basic investment principles and explore options based on your financial goals and risk tolerance. You may never have cared about this in the past, but if you're in charge now, make it your business to become informed. If you've always been in charge, review your investments with a trusted advisor on a regular schedule.

Emergency Planning & Funding: We've already discussed personal financial emergencies. These are a step above, but the principle is the same – being prepared can keep panic at bay. Develop a comprehensive emergency plan that includes contingencies for unforeseen events, such as job loss, economic downturns, or natural disasters. Having a plan in place can offset the impact of financial setbacks. You don't need to become obsessed with the worst possibilities. This could be as simple as knowing how to access your savings quickly or what to do if the fire alarm goes off.

Build an emergency fund to cover unexpected events. Aim for three to six months' worth of living expenses in a readily accessible savings. If that amount of money is impossible for you, learn about government assistance programs that may provide financial support during times of need. Investigate local community resources, religious institutions, charities, and nonprofits that assist individuals facing financial challenges. Some organizations offer emergency financial aid or resources to help with specific needs. Once you know what the supportive agencies are, keep their contact information along with your other financial paperwork. You may not need to apply now or ever, but if you know where to go and who to contact, you will feel more secure in an emergency.

Besides filing this information away, discuss it with a friend or someone you trust if that will give you more peace of mind. Someone else needs to know where to find this information when needed in case you need their help. You are preplanning to alleviate stress later.

THIRD LEVEL LIST

This last list is still important and will definitely take some time and effort. This is the final link in the chain that will make your future less stressful.

Estate Planning: The essential estate planning documents are a will, a durable power of attorney, and healthcare directives. Creating an estate plan is necessary to ensure that our wishes regarding the distribution of assets and healthcare decisions are clearly documented and legally binding.

Your Will: Most people are familiar with this. It's a legal document that reduces the potential for inheritance disputes. Your will should also include your last wishes about whether or not you want any specific funeral plans. When there are no family members to designate as beneficiaries in your will, there are other choices. Consider charitable organizations, friends or close associates, trusts or foundations, scholarship funds or educational institutions, medical research, or scientific causes. Without a will, the distribution of assets may be subject to probate, which can be time-consuming and costly.

Durable Power of Attorney for Healthcare: This is also known as a healthcare proxy. Suppose you cannot communicate or make decisions independently. In that case, you appoint an individual authorized to make medical decisions on your behalf. Healthcare decisions need to be carefully thought about and planned.

Advance Healthcare Directive: Also known as a living will, this document outlines specific healthcare preferences, treatment decisions, and end-of-life wishes. It is a legal document that provides guidance for your healthcare professionals. You can also communicate healthcare preferences and treatment decisions directly with healthcare providers. This can ensure that medical professionals are aware of your wishes and can work to honor those preferences. Additionally, you may want to wear a medical alert bracelet or carry a medical alert card that provides information about specific healthcare directives, allergies, or medical conditions. This can be particularly useful in emergency situations.

Regularly review and update these documents to reflect changes in your personal circumstances.

Exploring the bare bones of financial and legal preparations gives us a foundational framework for managing our economic future. Looking at the three priority levels helps us calmly analyze each step. When we break it down, the entire picture is not as overwhelming as the term 'financial planning' might seem. Financial and legal preparedness gives us autonomy over the ever-evolving landscape of our lives.

Let's revisit Carol Turner. We have yet to explore one important aspect of her story, which is her self-described agility and how she was able to develop it. She said she "turned to friends," and here's her quote, **"I'm quite fortunate to have a wonderful network from extended family, friends, and church community."**

A good part of her successful transformation into a Soloist was not due to financial planning at all. While financial planning is crucial for a secure future, reliance on support systems is equally important, adding a layer of resilience and emotional well-being to life. Support systems include a network of friends, family, mentors, and community connections that provide emotional and social support. In times of financial stress or uncertainty, having a reliable support system can give you guidance, a listening ear, and emotional comfort. Our support system becomes a source of encouragement during challenging periods and a cheering section for our victories.

Enjoy Life Without Financial Stress

Next, we'll look at our ability to fit what we want into the framework of our finances.

As humans, our desires are endless! And for a good reason. Without desire, humanity might still be living in caves. Desire is what propels the human race forward. We have invented and perfected our lives to this particular moment in time, where life offers us many opportunities to choose from.

Our capacity to want more also gets us into trouble. Many people learn the hard way that credit card spending is not the way to go about getting all the things we want. Hopefully, we are well beyond those hard-learned lessons. But we still have desires for physical things as well as emotional and social aspirations that go beyond basic human needs.

Understanding and addressing these desires with wisdom creates a fulfilling and well-rounded lifestyle. At this point in our lives, we may have concluded that happiness really doesn't lie in physical things. Our desires may be more along the lines of the emotional and social things. What we desire may fall under the category "The Best Things in Life Are Free" Or almost free.

According to Lifehack.org, there are three main categories that are most desired by Soloists. One of them is for companionship and connection. This includes close friendships, social circles, or romantic relationships that bring joy and a sense of emotional fulfillment. Here are three relatively easy ways to foster companionship and connection:

1. Joining social groups or clubs aligned with your interests is a straightforward way to connect with like-minded individuals. Whether it's a book club, fitness class, gardening group, or hobby-based community, participating in activities you enjoy increases the likelihood of meeting people with similar passions. Many communities have local meetup groups or online platforms where you can find information about gatherings related to your interests.

2. Volunteering provides a sense of purpose and an opportunity to meet new people who share your commitment to a cause. Choose a cause or organization that resonates with you, and dedicate some time to volunteering. Working alongside others for a common goal can naturally lead to meaningful connections. It could be a local animal shelter, community center, or environmental group.

Volunteering is a great way to make a positive impact while building connections.

3. Watch for community events and attend those that align with your interests. Is there a local fair, farmers' market, cultural festival, or neighborhood gathering? Community events provide a casual and welcoming environment for meeting people. Strike up conversations with neighbors, vendors, or fellow attendees to build connections within your community.

The key to creating companionship and connection is to be open, approachable, and proactive in seeking opportunities. Taking part in activities you enjoy or exploring new interests can naturally lead to building relationships with others who share similar values and passions.

The second top desire is for purpose and meaning in our lives. This often becomes more pronounced with age. We may seek opportunities for personal growth, contribution to society, or engagement in activities that bring a sense of fulfillment. Creating purpose and meaning in life is personal, but here are some easy ways to cultivate a sense of purpose. There is some overlap here because these two desires are closely related:

1. Engage in activities that bring joy and fulfillment. Explore hobbies or passions that have always sparked interest or discover new ones. Painting, gardening, writing, or learning a musical instrument, dedicating time to activities that resonate with personal interests can provide a sense of purpose and accomplishment.

2. Establish personal goals and challenges that provide direction and a sense of accomplishment. These goals can be diverse, including fitness milestones, learning new skills, or taking on personal projects. Break down larger goals into manageable steps and celebrate achievements along the way. Setting and achieving

personal goals contributes significantly to a feeling of purpose and progress.

The third top desire we might have is for health and well-being. We will be exploring this topic more fully in the next chapter. Here are two simple ways to foster health and well-being:

1. Engage in regular physical activity that suits your individual preferences and health conditions. This can include activities such as walking, swimming, yoga, or simple home exercises. Physical activity not only contributes to physical health but also promotes mental well-being and overall vitality. Start with activities that are enjoyable and gradually incorporate them into a routine.

2. Prioritize mental and emotional health through practices such as mindfulness, meditation, or deep breathing exercises. Find activities that bring joy and relaxation, such as reading, listening to music, or spending time in nature. Building a strong support network of friends, family, or even mental health professionals can provide outlets for expressing emotions and managing stress.

Are these the best things in life, and are they free? Depending on how much the things in the list above matter to us, we can devise ways to get or accomplish them whether or not we choose to pay for certain services like club or gym membership. Once we decide on what priority these things have in our lives, we can start planning how to go about getting them.

Most of these wants are subjects of self-help books, and if we're truly interested in what it takes to get to some of these desires, we might look for some books on these topics. Checking out books at the local library is free, as is borrowing books from friends – just don't forget to return them! Another option is used bookstores, which are relatively inexpensive, too. There's also the internet. A search will deliver a large amount of information on any subject.

As with any life choice, pursuing and accomplishing our aspirations is hugely satisfying and gives rise to increasing desire. If we are goal-setters, another milestone will probably appear, enticing us on to yet another goal. We can proceed through these nontangible goals, creating a very fulfilling life without too much concern for our budget.

Are we really done with wanting physical "things"? Of course not! Certainly, as Soloists, there are specific physical items or possessions we want. Some things are necessities, and some are desires that may remain on the shelf. One of the universal characteristics of desire for something is that we believe having it will enhance our comfort, convenience, and overall well-being. These wants can vary widely based on individual preferences, lifestyle, and priorities.

Here are some examples of physical things we may continue to want:

Comfortable Living Space: Desire for a comfortable and aesthetically pleasing living space filled with nice furniture, cozy bedding, and decor that reflects personal style. This comes with mortgage or rent payments and other price tags.

Travel and Gear to go with it: Do you have a "bucket list" of places you want to visit? Tourism usually takes planning to pay for it as well as to execute it. We may also want some things that go along with travel, such as luggage, travel accessories, or outdoor gear for those of us who enjoy adventure and exploration.

Hobbies and Creative Pursuits: Tools and equipment related to hobbies and creative pursuits can be pricy. This can be art or craft supplies, equipment, musical instruments, or gardening tools. Plus, there may be lessons or training that we need.

Fashion and Personal Style: We desire clothing, accessories, and items that reflect personal style and make us feel confident and comfortable in our appearance. There is usually a big price range here. High-end pieces can have astonishing prices attached.

Transportation: This usually means car payments, repairs, and insurance costs from low-end used cars to luxury models.

Some of the things in this list above are actually necessities. We do need shelter and clothing. Also, if public transportation is not available to you, then a vehicle and all its expenses are necessary. These physical items do cost money! Sometimes, a lot of money. Here is where we must devise a more strategic plan to get them. Fitting desired items into a fixed budget requires thoughtful planning and prioritization. Remember that budget we discussed in financial planning? We need it now. Assuming we have clearly identified fixed expenses like rent, utilities, etc., we know the amount of money we have to allocate to our list of desires over and above necessities. Discretionary spending is for things like entertainment, personal items, and treats.

Prioritize needs vs. nice-to-haves. It's okay to want something better than we have right now. These are goals. Daydream for a moment. Consider how much you want one thing over another. Make a list. There's no rush and no wrong choices. Once you have a Desire List, give each item a number. Decide if you want the number one item enough to make it a goal. If so, now you have something in mind to work toward.

Establish a clear amount of money you want to spend on a particular desire on your list. Choosing your top priority item and its estimated cost will guide your spending decisions from now on. This is the amount of money that needs to be carved out of the current budget. Here are ten ways to accomplish accumulating that amount in order for you to bring that desire into reality:

1. **Cut Unnecessary Expenses:** Review spending and identify areas where you can cut back. Eliminate non-essential expenses or find more cost-effective alternatives. This may involve reassessing subscription services, dining out less, or finding other creative ways to reduce costs.

2. **Pay off existing debt:** Stop using your credit cards or other charge accounts. Halting your debt from growing any larger can make it easier to manage. Not adding onto the balance while you're paying down debt can also help you create the extra money you want.

3. **Find a payoff method you'll stick with:** Paying off debt is a financial and psychological commitment. When you're dealing with paying down what you owe, you have to find a payoff method that works for you.

4. **Look into debt consolidation:** Debt consolidation is the process of combining multiple debts into one. This can make it easier to manage your debt and potentially lower your interest rate. Keep in mind this option does not reduce the amount you owe, but it can reduce your payments.

5. **Use Financial Assistance Programs:** Explore financial assistance programs or community resources that may be available to support specific needs. Some programs offer discounts or assistance for essential expenses like utility bills.

6. **Research and Comparison Shop:** When considering your desired item, shop around to find the best value for your money. Look for sales and discounts, and consider buying second-hand or refurbished items to save on costs. A better used car, for example, rather than a new one.

7. **Negotiate and look for Discounts:** Don't be afraid to negotiate or ask for discounts, especially for larger purchases. Many retailers are open to negotiations, and you may find opportunities to save money or get added value.

8. **DIY and Upcycling:** Consider do-it-yourself projects or upcycling to fulfill creative desires without breaking the budget. This can apply to home decor, fashion, and hobbies. DIY projects often provide a cost-effective and personalized approach.

9. **Plan for Deferred Gratification:** Adopt a mindset of deferred gratification. If a desired item doesn't fit into the current budget, find a way to save for it over time. This approach allows for more intentional spending and avoids impulse purchases.

10. **Regularly Review and Adjust:** Depending on how much you want what you want and how aggressively you can cut spending and increase saving, your desire might not take too long to materialize. Stay flexible and be willing to reassess priorities as needed.

Empower yourself with the ability to make financial decisions that align with your desires and fit seamlessly into your budget. Knowing your financial situation gives you stability. Balancing the area between needs and wants gives you control over your financial well-being. Set clear goals for your spending decisions with purpose and intent. Each thoughtful choice will fall into place. Adopting sound spending habits transforms your financial life into a controllable series of events rather than a situation that depends on luck. The result is a balanced budget and a lifestyle filled with the satisfaction of intentional choices. Your financial life is yours to design, and you have the power to shape it into a vibrant and prosperous future.

As we conclude our discussion on finances and estate planning, let's shift from contemplating the end of life to embracing the vitality of our present-day well-being and healthcare needs. In the upcoming chapter, we will explore strategies for maintaining optimal health and accessing quality healthcare services so we can lead fulfilling lives as Soloists.

***

THE TAILORED SOLUTIONS

Recognize and prioritize the essentials. Clarify and address financial and legal matters.

Arm yourself with the facts so you can live within your means.

Sustain an optimistic outlook. Honor your desires and work toward them.

Recognize and prioritize the essentials. Monitor your financial health to ensure long-term stability.

Ask for professional help when you need it. Get help from certified financial counselors or financial planners.

Look for the lessons you can learn. Soloists can be empowered to thrive by making informed decisions about personal finance.

CHAPTER 3

PRIORITIZE VITALITY - LIVE A VIBRANT LIFE

The letter "P" on the E.M.P.O.W.E.R Path stands for
Prioritize Vitality

These are fascinating times that we are living in now. Looking back to the year 1900, the life expectancy for white women was 48.7 years. A Black woman's life expectancy was a mere 33.5 years. Today, white women can expect to live until age 80.5 years and black women to age 76.1 years. The percentage difference in life expectancy has increased by approximately 65.26% for white women and 127.16% for black women from 1900 to today. These statistics symbolize the triumphs of advancements in healthcare and societal progress. They highlight the collective efforts made over the years to enhance the well-being of white women and a huge increase for black women. Although these statistics still do not express equality, they underscore the ongoing importance of healthcare initiatives, lifestyle choices, and public health policies in shaping a healthier and longer life.

Our health is the key to an abundant and fulfilling Solo Life. There is a great deal that we can do for our own health by being proactive. This chapter will address a few things we can do about maintaining our physical and mental health. As the statistics above show, we have come to expect more and want to experience the zest for life we anticipate. We'll look at healthcare, Medicare, and health maintenance as avenues to a thriving future.

Healthcare

A great healthcare experience depends on a great relationship with our primary healthcare physician. Your doctor is your medical "homebase." It's the doctor you visit for most medical needs, including wellness visits and routine screenings, non-emergency illnesses like earaches and sore throats, and the person you speak to about your health questions and concerns. Your primary care physician (PCP) may also be the person who refers you to see a specialist.

Some patient-primary care relationships can span decades, while others will be short-lived because you change insurance coverage or move out of the area. No matter how long you plan to see your PCP, the relationship is an important one. You'll want to find someone you feel comfortable having honest conversations with. It should be someone with expertise in the areas that meet your health needs. If, for any reason, you're not feeling that comfort level, be proactive about finding someone else. This is one area where you have total control.

Finding a New Doctor

Whatever the reason you might be looking for a different doctor, the process can be challenging. Several different types of doctors may be identified as primary care physicians, typically family practice, internal medicine, or general practice. Any of these doctors may refer patients to specialists if necessary.

Family Practice: Family practice physicians treat patients of all ages, from newborns to elders. They are generalists who can treat a wide variety of conditions and often can also treat ailments specific to women.

Internal Medicine: Internal medicine physicians typically treat adults and specialize in preventing, diagnosing, and managing disease and chronic conditions.

General Practice: General Practice physicians are like family physicians because they can treat patients of any gender or age. This category is one area where you might also find osteopaths, which are physicians who practice a type of alternative medicine with a special focus on the musculoskeletal system and are distinguished by the initials "D.O." (Doctor of Osteopathic Medicine) after their name instead of "M.D."

Ask for Referrals: Many people feel most comfortable visiting a doctor who is recommended by someone they know, like a family member, co-worker, or friend. Ask around and see who your friends and family visit when they have a health issue. You can also ask another healthcare professional with whom you have a relationship, like a pharmacist or even your dentist, for a recommendation. If you're moving, ask your current doctor if they have a recommendation for someone in your new location.

Think About Logistics: Do you want a doctor near your home or office? Search for doctors with an office location that is convenient for you to visit. You'll also want to consider office hours – what days and times does the doctor see patients? Will you need to take time off work to visit the office, or can you go after work or on weekends? It's also good to check which hospital the doctor uses to admits their patients. If you have to be admitted to a hospital, you want one you approve of and is relatively close to home.

Language is another important factor to check. You need to be able to communicate clearly with your doctor, so check which languages they speak to be sure you'll be able to understand each other. Many doctors now use email or an online portal to communicate with patients, which may be another item of importance if tech-savvy communications are an issue.

Visit the Doctor: Nothing can really give you a feel for whether you've selected the right doctor like an office visit and a face-to-face meeting. Be sure you feel comfortable in the office and with the staff. Be prepared to talk with your new prospective doctor about any current medications you are taking and your medical history to be sure you are both on the same page when it comes to managing any chronic conditions.

When in the office, notice your surroundings. Consider the demeanor of the people who answer the phone and greet you when you walk in – are they efficient and friendly? Are the phones answered promptly? And how long is the wait to see the doctor after you arrive for your appointment?

Medicare

Next up is a quick look at healthcare. Here again, many of us glaze over at first glance at this subject because the current US healthcare system is complicated! The following information on Medicare is also the bare bones version. Also, our healthcare systems may be changing. For now, Medicare is THE federal health insurance program created for individuals aged 65 and older and certain younger people with medical conditions or disabilities. Interestingly, not everyone 65 or older is required to enroll in Medicare. But it is a fact that if we don't enroll, there may be penalties.

Who would/could/should enroll? Most US residents are eligible for Medicare when they turn 65, but enrollment is not always mandatory at that age. Whether someone is required to enroll in Medicare depends on various factors, such as their current employment status and existing health coverage. You will need to find this information as it applies to you well ahead of time so you know what to expect.

Automatic Enrollment: If an individual receives Social Security benefits at least four months before turning 65, they are typically automatically enrolled in Medicare Part A (hospital insurance) and Part B (medical insurance). But, if you are not receiving Social Security benefits at the time you turn 65, you will need to actively enroll in Medicare. This can be done during the Initial Enrollment Period, which begins three months before you turn 65, including the month of your 65th birthday, and continues for three months after.

Employer-Sponsored Health Coverage: People who continue to work beyond the age of 65 and have employer-sponsored health coverage may choose to delay Medicare Enrollment without facing penalties. When their employer-sponsored coverage ends or when they retire, they can enroll in Medicare during a Special Enrollment Period without penalties.

Penalties for Late Enrollment: If someone does not enroll in Medicare when they are first eligible and they do not have qualifying health coverage through employment, they may face late enrollment penalties. These penalties can result in higher premiums for Part B and, if applicable, Part D (prescription drug coverage).

Anyone approaching the age of 65 should make an effort to understand their Medicare eligibility, whether they need to actively enroll, and the potential consequences of delaying enrollment.

Next, we wanted to know why it is so complicated. The complexity of the U.S. healthcare system, especially for Medicare, can be attributed to various factors.

Multiple Parts of Medicare: Medicare is divided into different parts (A, B, C, and D), each covering specific aspects of healthcare. Part A covers hospital care, Part B covers outpatient services, Part C (Medicare Advantage) combines Parts A and B and is offered by private insurance, and Part D covers prescription drugs. The existence of these multiple parts can lead to confusion regarding what is covered and how to navigate the system.

Eligibility Criteria: Eligibility for Medicare is based on age (65 and older) or certain disabilities. However, understanding the eligibility criteria, enrollment periods, and the implications of delayed enrollment can be confusing. Eligibility is not automatic for everyone, and individuals often need to actively enroll during specific periods.

Coverage Gaps: Despite comprehensive coverage, there are still gaps in Medicare coverage. For example, dental, vision, and long-term care services are not typically covered, leading many older folks to seek supplemental insurance or explore other options to fill these gaps.

Medicare Advantage Plans (Part C): The option of choosing Medicare Advantage plans, which are offered by private insurance companies, adds another layer of complexity. These plans may have different rules, coverage options, and costs compared to Original Medicare (Part A and B).

Prescription Drug Plans: Medicare Part D, which covers prescription drugs, involves choosing a standalone prescription drug plan or enrolling in a Medicare Advantage plan that includes drug coverage. The formularies, costs, and coverage rules for prescription drugs vary widely, making navigating challenging.

Supplemental Insurance (Medigap): Many beneficiaries opt for supplemental insurance to cover costs not paid by original Medicare. Choosing the right Medigap plan can be confusing due to variations in coverage and costs.

Changing Regulations and Policies: The healthcare landscape is dynamic, with regulations and policies constantly evolving. Changes in healthcare laws and policies can impact Medicare, leading to the need for beneficiaries to stay informed.

Provider Networks: Medicare Advantage plans, and some Part D plans often have provider networks, and understanding which healthcare providers are in-network can be difficult. This is particularly important for those who wish to continue seeing their preferred doctors.

Complex Billing and Coding: The billing and coding systems in healthcare are complex. Understanding bills, statements, and the various codes used can be hard to understand for anyone who is unfamiliar with the intricacies of healthcare billing.

Technology and Online Tools: Medicare communication and enrollment processes increasingly involve online tools and technology. Older adults who may not be tech-savvy can find it nearly impossible to navigate online platforms and understand the information presented.

One of the facts of life for anyone reaching the age of 65 is addressing these complexities. It often requires a combination of educational efforts, improved communication, and, hopefully, future policy changes to streamline and simplify the Medicare system for the older population.

Who can help us when we reach the point of being totally overwhelmed? Navigating the complexities of the U.S. healthcare system, especially Medicare, may require assistance. Thankfully, various professionals and resources exist:

Certified Medicare Counselors: Certified Medicare counselors, often available through State Health Insurance Assistance Programs (SHIPs), are trained to provide personalized assistance. They can help explain Medicare benefits, compare plans, and assist with enrollment. These counselors are typically unbiased and can provide guidance on various Medicare options.

Insurance Brokers: Licensed insurance brokers specializing in Medicare can help clients explore different Medicare Advantage and Medigap plans.

They can provide insights into various insurance options and assist in finding plans that best meet specific healthcare needs.

Health Insurance Counseling and Advocacy Programs (HICAP): HICAP programs are state-sponsored services that offer free and unbiased

Medicare counseling. They can help explain Medicare benefits, compare plans, and navigate enrollment processes.

Community Organizations: Local community organizations, senior centers, and nonprofit groups often provide educational sessions and workshops on Medicare. These sessions may offer insights into the system's complexities and provide guidance on making informed decisions.

Pharmacist Consultations: Pharmacists can provide information about prescription drug coverage under Medicare Part D. They can assist in understanding formularies, generic alternatives, and potential cost-saving strategies.

Healthcare Advocates: Healthcare advocates specialize in assisting with navigating the healthcare system. They can offer guidance on understanding bills, resolving disputes with healthcare providers, and advocating for the best possible care.

Online Resources: Trusted online resources like the official Medicare website have information and tools to help individuals understand their Medicare options. Online calculators and plan finders can assist in comparing different plans based on specific needs.

Financial Planners: Certified financial planners with expertise in retirement planning can help integrate healthcare costs into an overall financial plan. They can provide insights into budgeting for healthcare expenses during retirement.

Elder Law Attorneys: Elder law attorneys can provide legal advice related to healthcare decision-making, advance care planning, and issues related to long-term care. They can also provide guidance on Medicaid, which is a separate program from Medicare.

Family and Caregivers: Family members and caregivers can assist in researching options, attending appointments, and providing emotional support throughout the decision-making process.

None of this is simple or easy to understand, but help is available. Don't hesitate to find help when needed, and don't stop until you've found the answers to your questions. It's often a good idea to use a combination of these resources to ensure a comprehensive understanding of Medicare options and to make informed decisions based on individual needs and circumstances. Keep in mind that some resources in the list above are cost-free, but some charge fees, like financial planners and elder law attorneys.

Maintain Physical Health

Now, we can switch gears and begin looking at ways to maintain or improve our health. Let's look at Pam Peeke, MD, MPH, whose story appears on the website 10 Women Over Age 60 Who Inspire Wellness and Living Your Best Life.

> As a physician, scientist, and expert in preventive and integrative medicine, Pam Peeke has been at the forefront of educating people on how their diet and activity can help them lead long and vital lives.
>
> Beyond being an educator, at age 69, Peeke practices what she preaches as a triathlete in the National Senior Games, aka the "Senior Olympics." According to Peeke, who serves on the National Senior Games Association Foundation Board, "the average age of a Senior Olympian is 68," Peeke says, "but their average fitness age was 43. Their bodies tested to be similar to someone 25 years younger. So, if you want to whack a quarter century off your age, fitness and a healthy lifestyle is a great way to do it."

> As a Pew Foundation scholar in nutrition and metabolism and as an assistant professor of medicine at the University of Maryland, Peeke travels around the country trying to help people better understand the science behind living well in their later years. Her main message? It's never too late to get started.
>
> "Many of the people competing in the Senior Olympics weren't active for years. Life got in the way. They were raising children, holding down jobs. Now in their fifties and sixties, they are finding time to concentrate on themselves. They're less scared of taking on something new. It's never, ever too late to pick up full activity again. The benefits of doing it are exquisite."

As Pam suggests, "...if you want to whack a quarter century off your age, fitness and a healthy lifestyle is a great way to do it." so, let's look at that – exercise, diet, and mental health.

Exercise and Living

Changes in our bodies mean adjusting how we think about maintaining our health. Aging starts with our cells. As cells age, they function less well; eventually, old cells die, a normal part of the body's functioning.

The number of cells in our ovaries, liver, and kidneys decreases markedly as the body ages. When the number of cells becomes too low, an organ cannot function normally. This is why most organs function less well as people age. However, not all organs lose a large number of cells. The brain is one example. Healthy older people do not lose many brain cells. Substantial losses of brain cells occur mainly in people who have had a stroke or who have a disorder that causes the progressive loss of nerve cells, such as Alzheimer's disease or Parkinson's disease.

Most bodily functions peak shortly before age 30 and begin a gradual but continuous decline. However, despite this decline, most functions remain adequate because organs start with more functional capacity than the body needs. Even though most functions remain adequate, the decline in function means that older people cannot handle various stresses, including strenuous physical activity and extreme temperature changes in our environment. Diseases, not aging, usually account for most loss of function.

Osteoporosis is common in women. In this disease, there is an accelerated and pathological process of bone loss. Age-related bone loss occurs gradually over time as part of the natural aging process. Loss of bone density speeds up typically after menopause because less estrogen is produced. Estrogen helps prevent bone breakdown. Bones become less dense partly because they gradually contain less calcium, which gives bones strength. The amount of calcium decreases because the aging body absorbs less calcium from foods. Also, vitamin D levels, which helps the body use calcium, decrease slightly. The bones most affected include the end of the thighbone (femur) at the hip, the ends of the arm bones (radius and ulna) at the wrist, and the bones of the spine (vertebrae). The vertebrae become less dense, and the cushion of tissue (disks) between them loses fluid and becomes thinner, making the spine shorter. This is why older people become shorter. Regular weight-bearing exercises like walking, jogging, dancing, and strength training help stimulate bone formation and maintain bone density.

Osteoporosis is certainly a significant health concern for women. However, there are some other common health concerns, including cardiovascular disease, cancer, osteoarthritis, and depression, that we should be concerned about. Regular medical check-ups, healthy lifestyle habits, and proactive management of health conditions can help maintain optimal health.

Regular exercise to strengthen muscles can partially overcome or significantly delay the loss of muscle mass and strength. In muscle-strengthening exercises, muscles contract against resistance provided by gravity. Some beneficial exercises are sit-ups or push-ups and working out with weights or rubber bands. If this type of exercise is done regularly, even people who have never exercised can increase muscle mass and strength. Conversely, physical inactivity, especially bed rest during an illness, can significantly accelerate the loss. During periods of inactivity, older people lose muscle mass and strength much more quickly than younger people. For example, we would need to exercise for up to two weeks to compensate for the muscle mass lost during each day of strict bed rest.

The most significant bodily changes for women occur during menopause. The effects of aging on sex hormone levels are more evident in women than in men. When estrogen decreases dramatically, menstrual periods end permanently, and pregnancy is no longer possible. The decrease in female hormone levels causes the ovaries and uterus to shrink. The tissues of the vagina become thinner, drier, and less elastic. However, for most women, aging does not significantly detract from the enjoyment of sexual activity. In fact, not having to worry about becoming pregnant may enhance sexual activity and enjoyment.

One last fact we want to mention related to living longer is that the immune system reacts more slowly as we age. The immune system identifies and destroys foreign substances such as bacteria, other infecting microbes, and probably cancer cells. This immune slowdown may partly explain why cancer is more common among older people. Also, some infections, such as pneumonia and influenza, are more common among older people and result in death more often. Vaccines tend to be less protective in older people, but please remember that influenza, pneumonia, and shingles vaccines are essential and offer some protection.

On the positive side, allergy symptoms may become less severe. And, as the immune system slows down, autoimmune disorders become less common, such as Rheumatoid Arthritis (RA), Lupus Erythematosus (SLE), Inflammatory Bowel Disease (IBD), Psoriasis and Psoriatic Arthritis.

As we leave the slightly depressing descriptions of what happens to our bodies as we age, let's celebrate the remarkable resilience of the human body. Despite the challenges, our bodies have an incredible capacity to adapt, heal, and continue thriving in new and meaningful ways. Living longer brings a wealth of experiences and wisdom. Every wrinkle and gray hair tells a story of life lived, lessons learned, and challenges overcome. Embracing and honoring our past allows us to tap into a reservoir of knowledge that enriches us and those around us. As we face physical changes, we also uncover a reservoir of fortitude. Let's continue redefining what it means to be strong, recognizing that strength goes beyond our physical bodies and involves the depth of character we have developed with time.

Exercise is like a maintenance routine for our bodies. It's the practical tool that keeps everything running smoothly. Regular physical activity ensures our muscles stay strong, joints stay flexible, and stamina remains at its best. Think of it as a way to fine-tune the body's engine, helping us with the ups and downs of living longer. If you want to subtract 25 years from your age, as Pam Peeke suggests, start as soon as possible and stay with an exercise program. Let's keep moving because we're tuning our bodies for a robust future by continuing our everyday exercise routines.

Search on Amazon.com for books that will take you deeper into the subject of exercising specifically for your age bracket – 40's, 50's, 60's. You can find books on any exercise, from chair yoga to running marathons. Find YouTube videos that will demonstrate correct exercise techniques. Investigate your local YMCA, YWCA, health clubs, or fitness centers for in-person exercise classes.

Diet and Living

Armed with these positive thoughts, we'll take a quick look at what a healthy diet can do for us. Diet plays a significant role in health. The food we eat directly impacts life, influencing various aspects of the aging process.

Nutrient-rich foods provide essential vitamins, minerals, and antioxidants that support cellular health, which we know is essential. These compounds help protect cells from damage caused by free radicals contributing to aging and age-related diseases.

Chronic inflammation is associated with age-related diseases. A diet rich in anti-inflammatory foods, such as fruits, vegetables, and omega-3 fatty acids, helps reduce inflammation and support long-term health. Nutrients like vitamins C and E and zinc contribute to healthy skin. A well-balanced diet can help prevent premature aging of the skin, reduce the appearance of wrinkles, and promote a youthful complexion. As we have seen, adequate calcium and vitamin D intake are essential for maintaining bone health.

A diet low in saturated fats, cholesterol, and sodium contributes to heart health. Cardiovascular diseases become more prevalent with age, and a heart-healthy diet can help manage blood pressure and cholesterol levels. Maintaining a healthy weight is closely related to keeping our cardiovascular system running smoothly. A balanced diet, combined with regular physical activity, supports weight management and helps prevent obesity-related conditions that can impact aging.

An optimal diet for someone over the age of 40 should focus on meeting nutritional needs while addressing specific health considerations associated with aging. Two important considerations are dietary fiber from fresh fruits, vegetables, and whole grains. Fiber supports digestive health and helps maintain a healthy digestive system. Another factor is controlling blood sugar levels. Stable blood sugar levels contribute to overall health and can impact aging. Some studies suggest that certain dietary patterns, such as the Mediterranean diet, are associated with increased longevity and a reduced risk of age-related diseases.

Some Soloists may find that eating alone can be a very depressing situation. After years of shopping, cooking, and preparing food for a household, some of us are suddenly forced to scale back to preparing meals for one, and that can be a hard transition. If you find yourself in that situation, set a few ground rules. Don't skip meals. Skipping a meal undermines our good intention to eat well. If you're not hungry, eating a little is better than skipping a meal. Snacking is allowed. For most women over 50, it's best to eat three lighter meals and add two or three small snacks a day. Make meals a special time of day when eating well becomes an important part of self-care. You may even want to arrange an attractive table setting with tablecloth, napkins, nice dishes, and silverware. See how you feel about that. If it makes you happy, do it!

Search Amazon.com for books that will take you deeper into dieting specifically for your age bracket – 40's, 50's, and 60's. Watch your local events for upcoming diet and food-related programs. Local Senior Centers may have ongoing classes that might interest you.

Mental Health and Living

As we pay attention to the needs of our bodies through regular physical exercise and a well-balanced diet, let's not overlook the equally important area of our mental well-being. Living Solo extends beyond the physical and encompasses our mental and emotional well-being. Maintaining mental health is an important part of self-care. So, let's shift our focus from the physical to the cognitive, recognizing that a holistic lifestyle involves nourishing our bodies and minds.

Ensuring a good night's sleep is fundamental for mental health. Establish a consistent sleep routine, create a comfortable sleep environment, and limit stimulants before bedtime. Quality sleep enhances cognitive function, emotional resilience, and overall well-being. If you think your sleep could be better, try limiting screen time right before bed. The blue light emitted from electronic devices can interfere with the production of the sleep hormone melatonin. If you've already tried that, consult with a healthcare professional. There may be underlying issues, such as a sleep disorder or medical condition, that need attention.

Engage in activities that challenge the mind, such as puzzles, games, or learning new skills. Stimulating the brain promotes neuroplasticity, which can help maintain cognitive function and potentially reduce the risk of age-related mental decline. Doing puzzles or learning something new is fun and a great way to pass the time. Just like physical exercise strengthens the body, stimulating the mind through these activities fosters mental resilience and flexibility.

Maintain social connections by participating in group activities, clubs, or gatherings. Human interaction contributes to emotional well-being, reduces feelings of loneliness, and provides a support system during challenging times. Check out the local calendar of events in your community or at your local Senior Center.

Incorporate mindfulness practices, such as meditation or deep-breathing exercises, into your daily routine. Mindfulness promotes awareness of the present moment, reduces stress, and promotes mental clarity and emotional balance. Search the internet for more information on mindfulness practices, or stop by your local holistic center if there is one in your area.

Recognize the importance of seeking professional support when facing persistent mental health challenges. Therapists, counselors, and mental health professionals offer valuable insights, coping strategies, and a safe space to discuss and address any concerns. If you don't know where to go for help, start with your personal care physician. They are well aware of the resources near you.

Combining these practices into a holistic approach creates a foundation for emotional well-being and resilience when life throws out challenges.

Let's transition to the next chapter and consider the empowering possibilities of owning our identity. We will discuss building resilience and confidence as a natural extension of nurturing our mental health. We build a more resilient version of ourselves by embracing our uniqueness, facing challenges with courage, and fostering confidence. Each step forward shows our strength and capacity for growth.

***

THE TAILORED SOLUTIONS

Recognize and prioritize the essentials. Clarify and address your healthcare needs.

Maintain an optimistic outlook. A positive approach is an integral component of overall health.

Use stress-management techniques. Selecting appropriate healthcare for your needs can alleviate stress.

Maintain social connections. Human interaction contributes to well-being.

Develop a spiritual practice. Awareness of the present moment promotes mental clarity and emotional balance.

Ask for help when you need it. We have many options for healthcare advice.

CHAPTER 4

OWN YOUR IDENTITY - BUILD RESILIENCE AND CONFIDENCE

The letter "O" on the E.M.P.O.W.E.R Path stands for Own Your Identity

As we live longer, we can explore and understand who we are beyond society's stereotypes and expectations for Soloists. Let's take this time to explore self-identity and recall the unique experiences and wisdom that define us. We have a chance to redefine what it means to be a Soloist on our own terms. We can cultivate a positive self-image, appreciate our individuality, and challenge age-related stereotypes. Ultimately, this exploration contributes to personal growth and a broader cultural shift that encourages a more inclusive and empowered perspective on Living Solo.

Our identity constantly changes throughout life, but we might notice the most significant changes in our sense of self as we reach retirement age. At this point in our lives, our role in our family and community can shift dramatically, which leads to notable changes in the understanding of ourselves. "Age identity" is a common source of distress for Soloists. Why does this happen and, what can we do about it?

What is Identity?

Identity is a complicated mixture of roles, values, life experiences, and personality. It constantly changes as we enter new stages of life. We must often redefine what's important to us and who we are in relation to those redefinitions. As we live, we go through several significant changes that can impact how we understand ourselves and relate to the world. From a psychological viewpoint, personal identity is all about who you are - what makes - you. It includes how you see yourself, think about yourself, and feel about who you are. This sense of self develops over time, influenced by how you think, your relationships, and your experiences. It's not something fixed; it changes as you go through life. Your personal identity is a mix of beliefs, feelings, and perceptions, creating a unique sense of who you are.

Imagine being Debra.

> In the quiet corners of her once bustling city life, Debra, a resilient 60-year-old woman, found herself facing a profound transformation after a stroke rewrote the script of her existence. She was once a thriving insurance executive handling boardrooms with confidence. After the stroke, Debra was at the crossroads of reinvention as to who she was. The stroke had placed unexpected threads into the fabric of her identity, demanding that she relearn every nuance of life. The city that had witnessed her successes now became a place for rediscovery, a place where she must shape a new narrative. In the wake of this life-altering stroke, Debra discovered an unexpected truth — the desire to no longer continue the former life that once defined her. Instead, she took the opportunity to chart a different

> course, one that prioritized authenticity, and the quiet strength she found in rebuilding from the ground up. As Debra went through the uncharted territory of her post-stroke life, she became an inspiration for those who find themselves on unexpected journeys of reinvention, proving that in every twist of fate, there lies an opportunity for a new, fulfilling identity to emerge.

Our Changing Self-Identity

We change because our relationships with everything outside of us changes. As in Debra's story, for instance, when the stroke she suffered changed everything, everything about her life changed, and it happened all at once. Fortunately, most of us do not go through such dramatic life changes. Yet, our lives do change, and so must our identities. The evolution of our identity often hinges on three central pillars: our roles within our families, the status of our professional lives, and the core of our personal values. These elements fit together to shape a narrative of our lives. Let's take a closer look at these three pillars:

1. **FAMILY ROLES:** The role we play within our family is one of the biggest contributors to our sense of self. People with children derive a great deal of meaning from being a parent. If you have kids, you probably felt like a caretaker for years as your children grew up. Then, as your children became adults, you continued to be a source of advice and wisdom for them. When we age, though, we might need support from our children. The roles can reverse. Many older adults rely on their kids to some degree for transportation, financial assistance, or help with personal care. It can be jarring to go from being the caretaker to being the one needing help.

Becoming a grandparent can affect our identity as well. Welcoming a new generation into the world can be an incredibly exciting and meaningful experience, and many Soloists are very excited to take on their new role as a grandmother. Losing a spouse can also drastically affect our understanding of ourselves within a family structure. When partners have had years together, adjusting to life without them can feel almost impossible. If being a spouse is suddenly no longer a part of our identity, we may feel lost.

2. **PROFESSIONAL STATUS**: Retirement or losing a job is a massive life change and one of the most common causes of a shifting identity. While most Soloists are thrilled to retire and get extra time to enjoy life, putting a career behind you can also be very difficult if there is personal meaning in the work. Careers and jobs take up so much of our time that they usually contribute to our sense of self in some capacity. Even if we've been looking forward to retirement, we might feel like we've lost a big part of who we are. The sense of purpose and accomplishment from work can be very satisfying. After retirement, we have to find other projects and passions.

3. **PERSONAL VALUES:** Our sense of self includes our personal beliefs and values. In some ways, our identity may stay the same throughout our lives. The things we value most as young adults may continue to be meaningful to the present day. But we could also become more or less social, patient, or empathetic. We may value solitude more as we age or feel a new desire to surround ourselves with other people. Some people feel more connected to their emotional and mental health as they live longer. In contrast, others find that mental health gets more complicated to manage. Because life changes so much with age, our personalities and priorities may also change.

Coming to terms with age identity may feel difficult, especially if we've experienced a decline in health and rely on others for support. No matter our health status, though, we have the ability to accept our identity and feel at peace with who we are.

"Having a well-developed sense of self is hugely beneficial in helping us make choices in life. From something as small as favorite foods to larger concerns like personal values, knowing what comes from our own self versus what comes from others allows us to live authentically." - Erika Myers, a licensed professional counselor in Bend, Oregon.

Self-knowledge makes it easier to accept your entire self, both the traits you're proud of and those you'd like to improve. With self-awareness, addressing areas of dissatisfaction becomes more apparent because you possess a clearer understanding of your inherent traits and capabilities.

Lacking a clearly defined sense of self, on the other hand, often makes it challenging to know precisely what you want. If you feel uncertain or indecisive when it comes time to make important choices, you may struggle to make any choice at all. This often results in discontentment, even without identifiable issues or sources of unhappiness.

Awareness of personal values can go a long way toward understanding your sense of self. Values describe the traits you prioritize in yourself or others—empathy, honesty, trustworthiness, kindness, etc.

If you find it hard to make decisions, ask yourself, "Do my choices reflect my own interests or someone else's?" If you aren't sure how to answer this question, look at it from another angle: Would you make the same choices if you did not consider anyone else like a child, grandchild or friend? Decisions mostly grounded in your own desires and goals typically reflect a strong sense of self.

It might reassure you to learn it's not terribly uncommon to have a somewhat blurred sense of self. A 'fuzzy' sense of self happens quite normally in close relationships. It doesn't mean you've done anything wrong or that you're destined to live out your life without a clear identity.

It just indicates that you might want to look at that area of yourself more closely. Especially if you're now in a Solo Role.

Try these 3 strategies to begin establishing a more concrete, independent identity.

1. **Define your values:** Values and personal beliefs are fundamental aspects of identity. Your belief system can help you recognize what matters most to you and determine where you stand on important issues. For example, a desire to protect animal rights may lead you to choose cruelty-free products and make more informed choices about the foods you eat. Values can help guide the boundaries you set with others in your life. If you value honesty, for example, you might make it clear you can't maintain a friendship with someone who lies to you. You don't have to identify all your values at once, but try to think about what is important to you as you go about your day and interact with the world.

2. **Make your own choices:** Your decisions should, for the most part, primarily benefit YOU – your health and well-being. Suppose you have someone else in your life, for instance, a child or a parent. In that case, you will want to consider their opinions, though that shouldn't involve neglecting yourself. Remember, when your needs go unmet, you have less to offer others. Maybe you've let others make important decisions for you in the past — your choice of college, career, or where you live. If so, it might feel uncomfortable, even scary, to start making decisions for yourself. It's never too late to start, and it's OK to start small. Practice doing things because you want to do them, without asking for input from others.

3. **Value your time alone:** When you want to get to know someone, you spend time with them, right? It follows that getting to know

yourself better will involve some quality time alone. Take some time apart from others. Use this time however you like. If you'd really like to maximize self-exploration, try experimenting with things you can do alone, like reading, meditating, keeping a journal.

Once you have a more firmly defined sense of self, consider what you can do to align your life with your identity. You might ask yourself what changes you can make in your life or with others. It might feel overwhelming to begin defining your sense of self, especially if you've never given your identity much thought.

If you feel stuck, consider reaching out to a mental health professional for guidance. A therapist can offer support with emotional issues that relate to your sense of self, such as low self-esteem, depression, anxiety, or persistent unhappiness that stems from dissatisfaction with life. Even if you don't have any mental health symptoms, therapy is a great place to begin the self-exploration process. In therapy, you can identify values, uncover attachment issues or problematic relationship patterns, learn and practice decision-making skills, explore and address unmet needs, and work through anything related to self-image.

The concept of "self" isn't always easy to grasp, because identity naturally shifts and changes as time passes. It's normal to have some moments of confusion or self-doubt. When you consistently feel unfulfilled or struggle to name your needs and desires, consider taking the time for a bit of self-discovery.

Self-Confidence

Self-confidence is the belief in one's own abilities, qualities, and judgment. It is essential to a person's mental and emotional well-being, influencing how we approach challenges, interact with others, and navigate various aspects of life. Self-confident people typically have a positive and realistic perception of their capabilities, enabling them to set and pursue goals, handle setbacks, and engage in social interactions with assurance.

People with high self-confidence generally view themselves in a favorable light, acknowledging their strengths and accepting their imperfections. Self-confident people approach challenges with optimism. They believe in their ability to find solutions, learn from experiences, and adapt to changing circumstances.

Assertiveness is a key component of self-confidence. Confident individuals express their thoughts, feelings, and needs openly and respectfully, maintaining a healthy balance between self-assurance and consideration for others. Confidence is closely linked to courage. People with self-confidence are more willing to take calculated risks, step out of their comfort zones, and pursue their goals even when faced with uncertainty.

Self-confidence extends to social situations, allowing us to engage with others comfortably. Confident people can express themselves authentically, build positive relationships, and easily navigate social interactions. Self-confidence fuels motivation. Confidence allows us to set ambitious goals, stay committed to those goals, and persevere through challenges.

Going Solo usually means making our decisions independently. Self-confidence allows us to trust our judgment, make informed choices, and handle the challenges that may arise without constant external support. Being self-assured allows us to easily interact with others and enjoy social connections.

Solving problems confidently is very important for maintaining our independence. Sometimes, we must engage with various support services that come with living independently, such as our healthcare system, financial advisors, or home maintenance people. Self-confidence supports how we cope with daily interactions with others.

An effective strategy to cultivate and boost self-confidence is through the power of positive self-talk. When we consciously engage in self-talk, we are having a conversation with ourselves. This conversation can take various forms, such as analyzing a situation or reflecting on our thoughts and emotions. It allows us to process information, make sense of our experiences, and gain insights into our own beliefs, values, and motivations. The conversations we have with ourselves play a significant role in shaping our perceptions and responses to life's challenges. The art of positive self-talk is a powerful technique we can use to harness the strength within us and use it to build self-assurance.

On the other hand, negative self-talk can interfere with self-confidence. Try to steer clear of it. Catch yourself doing it and turn it around. By challenging distorted thinking patterns and replacing them with more constructive and realistic thoughts, we can transform negative internal dialogue and improve our self-confidence and mental health.

It's important to note that countering negative thoughts does not mean ignoring or suppressing them. Instead, it involves acknowledging and validating our emotions and thoughts while actively working towards reframing them more positively and constructively.

Here are more concrete activities we can do to build self-confidence:

- **STAY ACTIVE:** Exercise is one of the best ways to build confidence. Being active can also increase your opportunities for social interaction. Making connections can remind you that you're a fun person and a good friend. Endorphins, produced when we exercise, are neurotransmitters which are crucial in enhancing feelings of pleasure and well-being.

- **SPEND TIME WITH FRIENDS:** Quality time with loved ones is an excellent way to increase self-confidence. It's a reminder that you offer value to the people in your life and that your friends and family enjoy spending time with you. If you don't have many close friendships, try to expand your circle by reaching out to others. Everyone needs meaningful social interaction, and you're never too old to form new friendships.

- **INSTALL HOME MODIFICATIONS IF NEEDED:** If you're struggling with confidence because of difficulties moving around inside your home, installing modifications can help. Install handrails in the shower, invest in kitchen utensils that are easy to grip, and reorganize your home so that your most-used items are easy to reach. Almost all of us over 60 experience at least some loss in mobility and independence, but home modifications allow you to safely take care of your daily routines on your own.

- **VOLUNTEER:** Helping others boosts self-confidence. Volunteering is good for your community and provides you with a meaningful sense of accomplishment. It feels great to offer your time and energy to a worthy cause. Volunteering is a chance to make new friends and socialize, too. Use the internet to find volunteer opportunities in your area or check out your local library or community center to see if there are upcoming charitable events you could help.

- **SET GOALS:** You motivate yourself to learn and grow by setting practical, achievable goals. You'll feel great accomplishment when you reach the milestones, which can strengthen your self-confidence. If you have a hobby or talent, try setting small goals to improve that skill. For example, you could challenge yourself to read a certain number of books in a month or to participate in an art show to display your work.

- **TALK TO A THERAPIST**: Sometimes, self-criticism can become so severe that it's hard to overcome alone. If low self-esteem is getting in your way, seeking professional support might be the answer. Therapy can help break free from negative thinking habits. During counseling, you can learn how to turn that around.

Feeling confident in yourself can open up a whole world of possibilities. You'll feel less afraid to put yourself out there and meet new people and be proud to share your knowledge and talents with the world. High self-esteem empowers you to improve your social life and your physical health. Self-esteem is something you can work to build. By engaging in activities that help you feel good about yourself, you'll boost your confidence and gain a more positive outlook on life.

Resilience Matters

Resilience is the process and outcome of successfully adapting to difficult or challenging life experiences. It mainly shows up through mental, emotional, and behavioral flexibility. Resilience is a measure of how well we adjust to internal and external demands.

Resilience is not simply the ability to survive a difficult experience; it's the ability to adapt and cope in a way that enables us to emerge stronger. We grow through these difficult situations and thrive in the aftermath. Resilience lets us integrate lessons learned into a useful framework.

The Arizona Center on Aging at the University of Arizona developed a concept of resilience in aging known as a 'paradox of old age.' The paradox is that despite losses and physical declines experienced in later life, older adults report feeling content, and they have lower rates of psychopathology than the general population. Researchers argued that this is due to resilience and that an understanding of resilience can lead to ... healthier, happier people and communities.

The resilience of Soloists is marked by three key characteristics:
1. **Mental characteristics** including such things as adaptive coping styles, gratitude, happiness, mental health, and optimism/hopefulness.

2. **Social characteristics,** like community involvement, contact with family and friends, a sense of purpose and strong, positive relationships.

3. **Physical characteristics** centered around the ability to remain

physically independent and mobile, enjoy good health, and the belief that one is aging successfully.

Learning the behaviors of resilient living will increase our ability to cope with difficult circumstances.

As you repeatedly focus on practicing what you can do to overcome challenging circumstances, you may soon find that it becomes second nature, leading you toward a more empowered, engaged, happy, and, yes, resilient life.

Our discussion of identity, self-confidence, and resilience has set a foundation, positioning us to transform aging stereotypes into living flexibility. By developing the many layers of self-identity, we challenge the stereotypes that often accompany aging. We can set our own benchmark that celebrates the diversity, strength, and individuality of our Solo Lives. In the next chapter, we will see how this foundation sets us up to build and maintain our relationships.

***

THE TAILORED SOLUTIONS

Maintain an optimistic attitude and always look for the best outcome.

Practice stress-management techniques. Relying on your own self-confidence reduces stress.

Make self-care a priority. You will have more to give to others when you pay attention to your own needs.

Volunteering your time to help others builds self-confidence.

Ask for help when you need it. Therapy has many advantages.

Look for the lessons you can learn. Your attention to responding with confidence demonstrates growing resilience.

CHAPTER 5

WOVEN BONDS - BUILD AND MAINTAIN RELATIONSHIPS

The letter "W" on the E.M.P.O.W.E.R Path stands for Woven Bonds

As we have seen in previous chapters, Soloists may depend heavily on our social network. If family or extended family is not available to us, friends, neighbors, and community ties may be our only support system. Building and maintaining these social connections becomes very important.

Community

Community involvement gives us a sense of belonging and purpose. Engaging in activities, clubs, or volunteer work provides opportunities for social interaction and contributes to a meaningful and fulfilling daily life. Being part of a community allows us to share experiences, exchange knowledge, and celebrate achievements. Community holds our sense of connection and shared identity.

Here's the story of Barbara, a vibrant 70-year-old woman who enthusiastically embraces being a Soloist.

> Barbara lives in a tight-knit neighborhood where she has cultivated meaningful connections over the years. One day, she faced a health challenge that required some immediate attention.
>
> Instead of navigating this situation alone, Barbara relied on her network of friends and neighbors. A close friend, Sarah, helped coordinate rides to medical appointments, making sure Barbara received necessary care without the added stress of finding transportation. Another neighbor, Mike, helped out with grocery shopping so that Barbara had good meals during her recovery.
>
> Beyond practical support, the emotional backing Barbara received from her community is invaluable. Cards, well-wishes, and visits from neighbors continue to uplift her spirits, reinforcing that she is not alone in facing life's challenges. Social connections played a crucial role in her recovery, providing companionship and preventing feelings of isolation.

This scenario underscores how community and social connections create a safety net. In times of need, having a network that offers both practical assistance and emotional support enhances the overall well-being and resilience of those like Barbara, making Solo Living more manageable and fulfilling.

Social Connections

Our social connections are a vital aspect of well-being. They provide emotional, physical, and cognitive benefits. Forming and maintaining these connections is essential for a positive and fulfilling Solo Life. The opposite of social connection is isolation and loneliness, which are almost as dangerous as lifelong tobacco and alcohol use and are even more detrimental to our health than morbid obesity or a complete lack of physical activity. People with strong social connections in their later years have nearly a 50% greater chance of living longer. As we can see in Barbara's case, the help of her community was very important to her recovery.

Here's an analysis of the ways she was supported:

Emotional Support: Having a network of people to share experiences helped her deal with the stress associated with her health crisis.

Loneliness and Isolation: Social connections offered companionship and a sense of community, mitigating the negative effects of isolation on her mental and emotional health.

Physical Health Benefits: Research suggests that strong social connections can have positive effects on physical health, which helped Barbara's recovery. Soloists with robust social networks experience lower rates of chronic diseases, improved immune function, and better overall health outcomes.

Cognitive Stimulation: Engaging in social interactions provided Barbara with cognitive stimulation, essential for maintaining mental sharpness and preventing cognitive decline. Interacting with others, sharing ideas, and having conversations contribute to cognitive well-being.

Practical Support: The people she was connected to offered practical assistance, such as help with daily tasks, transportation, and other needs. This support becomes increasingly important the longer we live.

Quality of Life: Ultimately, Barbara's quality of life was significantly influenced by the strength of her social connections. Meaningful relationships, a sense of belonging, and a supportive community contribute to a more fulfilling and enjoyable Solo Experience.

Increased social connection also has these physical effects on the body:

- Increased cardiovascular health.

- Lower blood pressure and reduced hypertension.

- Decreased risk for certain cancers, osteoporosis, and rheumatoid arthritis.

Adults with healthy social lives, especially women, have lower levels of the inflammatory proteins interleukin-6 and C-reactive, which cause chronic inflammation throughout the body, including the brain.

Creating and maintaining healthy social relationships is our foundation for a vibrant and fulfilling life.

Consciously Creating Connections

What if we don't have a close social network close by like Barbara? We have 2 alternatives – start building one now or move into an existing one. Both ways offer unique opportunities for connection and community. Each option presents its own set of challenges and rewards, but the goal remains the same: to cultivate meaningful relationships and create a sense of belonging.

If you start building a social network from scratch, it will be like planting seeds in fertile soil. This approach requires patience, effort, and a willingness to actively seek out opportunities to make it grow. By engaging in activities such as joining community groups, attending social events, or volunteering, we're sowing the seeds of potential friendships and social bonds. While it may take time for these connections to blossom, the process of nurturing new relationships can be incredibly rewarding and enriching.

On the other hand, you could choose to move into an existing social network, like a retirement community. There, your experience would be like planting yourself in a thriving garden where everything is already in place for you. Retirement living communities offer a supportive and inclusive environment where residents can build meaningful connections, and friendships, and enjoy a fulfilling social life. Community activities and opportunities for socialization will already be organized for you to join. Many people thrive and find a sense of belonging within a retirement community.

Let's follow these 2 routes to see how either one might work out. Regardless of which route you take, the key is to be proactive in building and maintaining those valuable social connections. Both ways will work if you are willing to make an effort to participate in community groups, attend social events, or volunteer your time.

Route #1 The DIY Method

Join Community Groups or Clubs: Look for organizations that align with your interests or hobbies. Whether it's a book club, gardening group, or volunteer organization, participating in activities can help you meet like-minded individuals and form new social connections.

Attend Social Events: Watch for social events or gatherings in your area, such as town hall meetings, art exhibits, or cultural festivals. These events provide opportunities to interact with others and potentially forge new friendships.

Take Classes or Workshops: Enroll in the ones that interest you. Not only will you gain new skills and knowledge, but you'll also have the chance to connect with classmates and instructors on a social level.

Use the Internet: Explore online platforms to find communities that connect people with shared interests or backgrounds. Websites like Meetup, Facebook Groups, or forums related to your interests can be valuable resources for meeting new people and forming relationships.

Attend Groups: Find live, in-person Meetup events in your area that cater to your specific interests or demographics. Find them at https://www.meetup.com/. Meetup offers a wide range of activities and gatherings where you can meet new people and expand your social circle.

Volunteer: Volunteering is one of the most beneficial activities for Soloists. Consider volunteering for local charities, nonprofit organizations, or community initiatives. Volunteering provides a sense of fulfillment and purpose. It allows you to connect with others who share your values and commitment to making a difference.

Initiate Social Outings: Be proactive and organize social outings or gatherings with acquaintances or neighbors. It could be a casual coffee gathering, a movie night, or a potluck dinner. Hosting events can help build connections and create opportunities for bonding.

Attend Networking Events: Go to meetings or professional mixers related to your career or industry. These events provide opportunities to meet new people, expand your contacts, and form personal and professional relationships. Many professional groups welcome retirees who might be willing to share the wisdom they've gained over the years in presentations at their meetings. Another possibility might be to mentor younger people who are just starting out in your particular field.

Building strong social connections takes time and effort, so be patient and persistent in pursuing meaningful relationships. Be prepared to step out of your comfort zone and try new activities or approaches to meet people. You can create strong bonds if you have an open mind and a willingness to connect.

Route #2 The Ready-made Method

Joining a retirement community can offer a ready-made social network and a supportive environment for those who want to connect with others in a similar stage of life. Here's how it could work out:

Community Activities and Events: Retirement living communities often organize a variety of activities and events designed to foster socialization and community engagement. These may include group fitness classes, book clubs, arts and crafts sessions, movie nights, and outings to local attractions. By participating in these activities, residents can meet and interact with their neighbors, forming friendships based on shared interests.

Common Areas and Facilities: Many retirement communities feature common areas and facilities where residents can gather and socialize. This may include community centers, lounges, libraries, game rooms, and outdoor spaces like gardens or walking trails. These spaces serve as hubs where residents can mingle, chat, and get to know one another in a relaxed and welcoming environment.

Interest-Based Groups: Within retirement communities, residents often form interest-based groups or clubs centered around shared hobbies, passions, or activities. These groups might focus on gardening, photography, cooking, or music interests. Joining these groups allows residents to connect with like-minded people who share their enthusiasm for a particular interest.

Supportive Atmosphere: Retirement living communities, by nature, provide a supportive environment where residents can lean on one another for companionship, assistance, and emotional support. Whether lending a listening ear, offering practical help with tasks or errands, or simply sharing a meal or conversation, residents can rely on their neighbors for friendship and camaraderie.

Community Dining: Many retirement communities offer dining options where residents can enjoy meals together in a shared dining room or restaurant-style setting. These mealtimes provide:

- Opportunities for residents to socialize over food.

- Swapping stories.

- Sharing laughter.

- Building connections with their fellow community members.

Resident-Led Initiatives: Residents often take the lead in organizing social activities, outings, or events within the community. This might include hosting potluck dinners, organizing game nights, planning day trips, or celebrating holidays and special occasions together. These activities contribute to a vibrant and dynamic social atmosphere within the community.

Retirement communities offer a supportive and inclusive environment where residents can build friendships and enjoy a fulfilling social life. By actively participating in community activities, engaging with fellow residents, and taking advantage of the opportunities for socialization, residents can thrive and find a sense of bonding within their retirement community.

Making the Choice

Choosing between creating your own community and joining a ready-made retirement community involves considering several factors, including personal and lifestyle preferences, practical considerations, and social needs. Here are some things to consider when making this decision:

Social Preferences: What is your level of desire for community engagement? If you enjoy meeting new people, participating in group activities, and being part of a larger community, joining a ready-made retirement community may be the ideal choice. On the other hand, building your own local community might be more appealing if you prefer a more intimate setting or have a specific vision for the community you want to create.

Your Lifestyle: Consider your tastes and the things you like and dislike. Ready-made retirement communities often offer a range of amenities, such as fitness centers, dining options, recreational activities, and social events. If these amenities align with your lifestyle preferences and needs, joining a pre-existing community may be the best option. However, if you have specific preferences or requirements that are not met by an existing community, creating your own community allows you to tailor the environment to suit your preferences.

Location: Consider the location of a potential retirement community and how it aligns with your lifestyle and preferences. Ready-made retirement communities may be located in urban, suburban, or rural areas, each offering different advantages and amenities. Evaluate factors such as proximity to family and friends, access to healthcare services, climate, recreational opportunities, and cost of living when choosing a location. Staying where you are offers the advantages of familiarity and access to established services and amenities. Your current location may give you more sense of comfort, independence, and continuity, allowing you to maintain your lifestyle while remaining in place.

Cost: There's a lot to consider here. Several factors emerge when considering what either option will cost. These will be mainly related to financial savings, flexibility, and customization.

- Staying where you are and building a strong social network can be more cost-effective than moving into a retirement community. By remaining in your current home, you avoid the significant upfront costs associated with relocation, such as entrance fees, moving expenses, and potential real estate transaction fees. Additionally, you may be able to maintain lower living expenses by staying in a home where the mortgage is already paid off or where your mortgage payments are lower than the monthly fees associated with a retirement community. Staying where you are can result in long-term cost savings and financial stability.

- Remaining in your current location gives you greater flexibility and independence in structuring your living arrangements and lifestyle. You can customize your living space according to your preferences and needs, whether that involves modifying your home for staying in place or downsizing to a smaller residence in the same area. Independent living allows you to control your living environment and make decisions that align with your values and goals.

- Staying in your current location, you have the opportunity to cultivate a social network that is tailored to your interests, preferences, and values. You can actively engage with your existing community, participate in local events and activities, and build meaningful relationships with neighbors, friends, and community members. This personalized approach to social connection allows you to foster deeper, more authentic relationships based on shared interests and experiences. Additionally, you have the flexibility to expand your social circle at your own pace and in ways that resonate with you rather than adhering to the social dynamics of a retirement community.

Remaining where you are and creating a strong social network offers advantages in terms of cost savings, flexibility, and tailored social connections. These factors provide a compelling case for continuing in place and maintaining independence while making those meaningful relationships within your existing community.

However, there are potential cost benefits associated with moving into a retirement community, depending on individual circumstances and preferences. Here are several cost-related advantages of moving into a retirement community:

- Many retirement communities offer a bundled package of services and amenities included in a monthly fee or entrance fee. These amenities may include maintenance-free living, utilities, housekeeping, lawn care, transportation services, security, and access to recreational facilities such as fitness centers, swimming pools, and community centers. By bundling these services together, residents can often enjoy cost savings compared to paying for them separately in a traditional home setting.

- Moving into a retirement community can provide greater predictability and stability in monthly expenses. Instead of managing all the bills and costs associated with homeownership, such as property taxes, home insurance, utilities, maintenance, and repairs, residents pay a monthly fee that covers most or all of their living expenses. This predictability can help with budgeting and planning for retirement without worrying about unexpected costs or fluctuations in expenses.

- For those selling their primary residence to move into a retirement community, there may be cost benefits associated with eliminating homeownership expenses. Selling a home can free up equity and reduce ongoing costs such as mortgage payments, property taxes, homeowner's insurance, and maintenance expenses. By transitioning to a retirement community, it's possible to redirect the funds previously allocated to homeownership toward their retirement lifestyle and priorities.

- Some retirement communities offer access to healthcare services and support as part of their continuum of care. This may include on-site medical facilities, assisted living, memory care, or skilled nursing care, depending on the level of care needed. By residing in a retirement community with integrated healthcare services, residents can save on future healthcare costs and avoid relocation to a different care setting as their needs change over time.

- As mentioned, retirement communities often provide a wide range of social, recreational, and cultural activities and events for residents to enjoy. These activities may be included in the monthly fee. They can contribute to residents' overall well-being and quality of life. By participating in on-site activities and events, residents may save on entertainment and leisure expenses that they would otherwise incur outside of the community.

It's important to carefully evaluate the costs and benefits of retirement community living. Consider potential retirement communities' values, culture, and atmosphere and how well they align with your preferences and priorities. Research the community's mission, vision, and values, and visit the community to understand its culture and atmosphere. Choose a community where you feel comfortable, welcomed, and aligned with the values and culture. Take the time to carefully evaluate each option, weigh the pros and cons, and consider how each choice aligns with your lifestyle, social needs, and long-term goals for your retirement.

The Ties That Bind

Now that we have carefully considered the factors involved in choosing our community, we will look at the best ways to maintain our all-important human connections. Building a sense of camaraderie, support, and mutual respect among neighbors enriches our daily lives. It contributes to the vibrancy and cohesion of our community as a whole.

Our emotional well-being hinges on our ability to forge and sustain robust bonds with others. Feeling connected and supported reinforces our confidence and equips us to deal with life's challenges with greater resilience. However, relationships require care to flourish. They thrive through a give-and-take process and need attention. Fortunately, a wealth of tried-and-true methods exist to nurture existing relationships and form new ones.

Stay Connected: Make an effort to stay in touch with friends regularly wherever they may be. Communicate through phone calls, video chats, emails, or handwritten letters. Set aside time for catch-up sessions, virtual coffee dates, or outings to stay connected and maintain communication.

Get together: Take advantage of opportunities to be together in a relaxed and social setting. Don't hesitate to initiate plans or extend invitations to friends for coffee, lunch, or outings.

Be a Good Listener: Practice active listening and empathy when interacting with friends. Be genuinely interested in their lives, experiences, and concerns, and offer support and encouragement when needed. Being a good listener strengthens trust and deepens emotional connections.

Show Appreciation: Express gratitude and appreciation for your friends regularly. Take the time to acknowledge their kindness, support, and presence in your life. Small gestures such as sending a thoughtful note, bringing homemade treats, or offering a heartfelt compliment can strengthen bonds and reinforce the value of your relationship.

Be Reliable and Supportive: Be the best friend you can be by offering assistance, encouragement, and companionship when needed. Lend a helping hand or a listening ear during challenging times. Provide practical help or emotional support if needed. Demonstrating reliability and supportiveness builds trust and strengthens relationships over time.

Celebrations: Celebrate milestones, achievements, and special occasions with your friends. Birthdays, anniversaries, or personal accomplishments, take the time to acknowledge and celebrate these moments together. Plan gatherings, outings, or small parties to commemorate these occasions and strengthen your bonds.

Boundaries: Respect the boundaries and preferences of your friends, recognizing that everyone has different needs and priorities. Be mindful of their time, energy, and personal space, and avoid imposing or overstepping boundaries. Respectful communication and mutual understanding contribute to healthy and sustainable relationships.

Prioritize Yourself: Prioritize self-care and personal well-being to ensure you have the energy and emotional resilience to nurture others. Take time for activities that recharge and rejuvenate you, such as exercise, hobbies, meditation, or spending time in nature. By prioritizing self-care, you'll be better equipped to show up as a supportive and engaged friend in your relationships.

Be Open to New Friendships: Stay open to expanding your social circle. Be proactive in meeting new people and initiating conversations, whether it's at community events, classes, or social gatherings. Take advantage of opportunities to connect with others and cultivate new friendships based on shared interests and values.

Dating

We need to quickly change our focus for a moment. While we have been primarily looking at platonic relationships, it's worth noting that for some, dating may also play a significant role in their social landscape. Dating can be a source of excitement, adventure, and renewed vitality. It provides a chance to connect, share experiences, and cultivate meaningful relationships that bring joy and fulfillment. If your circle of close relationships includes dating, so much the better. All of the people in our lives are important. A significant other is always an addition to our lives.

Let's clarify that the focus of this book is not on dating or romantic relationships. This chapter has focused on providing guidance on cultivating strong relationships in general. Given the depth and complexity of the topic of dating, there are many dedicated resources available that go into this aspect of social life more comprehensively. While we recognize the importance of significant personal relationships, our primary focus here is on building a strong, supportive social network as Soloists.

Coming up, we turn our attention to another essential aspect of Solo Living - discovering new passions and hobbies. While relationships provide companionship and support, cultivating personal interests and engaging in fulfilling activities adds depth and richness to our lives. Finding new interests sparks creativity and curiosity and gives us a sense of delight in the moment. Discovering new interests opens exciting new avenues for enjoying life.

***

THE TAILORED SOLUTIONS

Maintain social connections. Friends and neighbors can provide emotional and practical support.

Recognize and prioritize the essentials. Clarify your ideal living situation and the benefits of community involvement.

Engage in new activities. Participating in community builds mutual support.

Cultivate new connections. Our relationships give us a fulfilling Solo Lifestyle.

Volunteer your time. Use volunteering as a way to engage with the community.

Ask for help when you need it. Reach out to your community of friends.

An Easy Way You Can Help Someone Else

"Communication is merely an exchange of information, but connection is an exchange of our humanity." — Sean Stephenson

> Sean Stephenson (1979-2019) was a motivational speaker, author, and therapist known for his inspiring messages and unique perspective on overcoming life's obstacles. Born with osteogenesis imperfecta, a rare bone disorder that stunted his growth and caused fragile bones, Stephenson faced numerous physical challenges throughout his life. Despite these, he became a powerful advocate for self-empowerment and resilience.

Thank you for exploring the E.M.P.O.W.E.R. PATH with us so far. Your journey through this book can be more than a personal exploration. It's an opportunity to spread the network of connection to others navigating the complexities of Aging Solo.

Your unique perspective and experiences are invaluable, and by sharing your thoughts, you can help others discover the guidance, support, and inspiration they need to embrace their own Solo Journey.

Your review matters. It's a beacon of light for those seeking guidance, assurance, and companionship on their Solo Aging path. Your words can show the way forward for others, offering them the strength of knowing they're not alone in their journey.

As Sean Stephenson beautifully articulated, "Communication is merely an exchange of information, but connection is an exchange of our humanity." By leaving a review for this book, you will be extending a helping hand to fellow Solo Agers, guiding them toward a resource that could enrich their lives in profound ways.

Thank you for your willingness to share your thoughts. Together, we can expand the knowledge that everyone can thrive while Aging Solo.

Click on the book cover image or use the link or QR code below to leave a review.

htttps://www.amazon.com/review/create-review/?ie=UTF8&channel=glance-detail&asin=B0D3FQC78K

CHAPTER 6

ENERGIZE YOUR ESSENCE - DISCOVER NEW PASSIONS

The Second letter "E" on the E.M.P.O.W.E.R Path
stands for Energize Your Essence

Embracing change and pursuing new interests can significantly rejuvenate the spirit. In this chapter, we will see how discovering and engaging in new passions and hobbies can lead to a revitalized zest for life.

Our hobbies bring us joy and help improve mood at any age, but it's especially important for those of us over 60 who have the luxury of additional free time. When we find ourselves feeling stuck in a daily routine, engaging in a hobby can increase overall happiness and satisfaction with life.

> Let's take a look at the legendary Julia Child. She is quoted as saying, "I was 50 years old when I started cooking; I had plenty of time to enjoy the pleasures of good food and the art of cooking." As the famously adored chef, author, and television personality, Julia

> Child is a familiar name in the homes and hearts of Americans to this day. But she wasn't always known for her delicious recipes and humorous dialogue. Julia did not decide to learn how to cook until after pursuing her career in media and advertising. She took cooking classes while living in France and turned her newfound hobby into a totally new career as a celebrity chef with her own TV show. She also became the first woman to be inducted into the Culinary Institute of America's Hall of Fame.

We know that age is not a barrier to doing what we love or finding something new to ignite us. Julia Child found her passion for cooking, and it opened a new, fulfilling, and enriching pursuit. We can tap into our unique interests and aspirations and increase our enthusiasm for life.

"Energizing your Essence" means more than simply finding a new hobby. The essence of who we are—our creativity, curiosity, and sense of adventure is triggered by doing things that bring us alive and spark the imagination. What pulls that trigger will be different for everyone. It could be immersing ourselves in the beauty of nature, expressing ourselves through art or music, exploring the world of literature, or any other interest that seizes our attention.

Energizing our essence means connecting with the things that make us feel most alive and vibrant.

Avocation

Good things happen when we engage in an activity we've always loved or discover something new. We uncover or enhance hidden talents, overcome challenges, and unlock new potential. The tangible benefits are that engaging in a hobby brings stress relief, a boost to the immune system, and improved cognitive abilities.

These pursuits light up our lives and bring us closer to living our most authentic selves. If you've had this experience, it feels like life itself is pulling us forward. It could be defined as an avocation or calling that we can hardly resist. Some people describe it as a state of "flow," where we feel completely immersed in the present moment, effortlessly absorbed in what we are doing. In this heightened state of concentration and enjoyment, it's as if we are in touch with a powerful life force that gives us a sense of purpose and vitality. Once experienced, this sensation is unforgettable and often motivates us to continue that activity because the avocation has become part of our essence.

How do we find this kind of leisure pursuit? Welcome to a world of endless possibilities! Let's revel in the fact that the rest of our lives are brimming with opportunities to discover the best ways to use our time. With each passing moment, we have the chance to uncover new passions, explore uncharted territories, and play with the joy of life's adventures. Imagine igniting with anticipation and enthusiasm as we set out to unlock what the future holds. We have no limits, and adventure is waiting!

Start the discovery process by reflecting on topics or activities that have always intrigued you. It could be anything, such as learning a new language or writing poetry. Don't hesitate to step out of your comfort zone and experiment with different activities until you find one that resonates with you. Consider joining community groups or centers that offer activities of interest to you. Dabble. Try lots of things.

Next, anticipate discovery. Look at this as an opportunity to grow, but don't let the pressure to find your perfect avocation right away derail you. It's a learning process, so give yourself some time, have fun, and experiment along the way.

One suggestion about discovering your passion is to dive into your past. Reflect on what brought you joy and a sense of fulfillment when you were younger. Did you enjoy playing a certain game or sport? Perhaps you loved gardening, reading, or playing a musical instrument. Think about things you've always wanted to try but never had the time. Your younger self can provide inspiration for interesting things to revisit.

Whether they realize it or not, most people are drawn to particular subjects: foods, books, movies, TV shows, and even types of people. Think of those things as "themes" and explore what attracts you to them and how you might expand those themes going forward. Talk to your friends and family. If you need help zeroing in on what your interests are, ask those who know you best what they think. They will likely point out your frequent topics of conversation or areas that they've seen you get excited about. Sometimes, we don't even realize how we like to spend our time. Look back on activities you naturally choose. Notice what television shows you watch or books you read. See if there is a pattern you can capture. This could be your key to defining a passion.

The journey of life can take us down many roads, and along the way, we may find we had to leave behind personal interests so we could concentrate on more pressing tasks. Living longer often returns the opportunity to finally have time to spend as you like. You may decide to start a second career and put your efforts toward an area of life you may have missed. It could be giving politics a try and running for a local office. What about becoming a kindergarten teacher because you once dreamed about working with little ones? You have the time now to recapture those lost opportunities. Think back to your earlier dreams.

Volunteering might be your passion. For many, nothing warms your heart more than helping someone else. It can certainly give you purpose and can quickly become a passion. To find your cause, research local charitable organizations you're already familiar with or connect with online volunteer matching services like VolunteerMatch and SeniorCorps.

Lifelong Learning

Browse through a college course catalog. This can be a wonderful place to jumpstart your search for a meaningful hobby if you need guidance. You don't need to sign up for a class, although you might. Look for any subjects that pique your interest and let your imagination explore. Keep an open mind, and don't reject any initial ideas because you assume they're not passion-worthy. Be willing to investigate different options. You might discover something about yourself that has gone unnoticed. Browsing through college catalogs can serve as a reminder that learning is a lifelong process that extends far beyond the confines of formal education. Exploring the options from nearby colleges can lead you to just what you've been looking for.

Learning itself may become an avocation. Remember when learning was a task or obligation, as when we were trying to prepare for a career? Now, it can become a source of inspiration, curiosity, and personal growth. Every new subject we investigate deepens our understanding of ourselves and the world around us.

Living longer doesn't mean we stop growing our minds. There are cognitive benefits in lifelong learning. Studies show that participating in educational programs of any type can improve memory and minimize cognitive decline by stimulating more significant neuron generation in the brain. There are also physical benefits to learning, such as reduced muscle tension and blood pressure, and decreased depression.

Continued learning exposes us to new ideas, cultures, and perceptions. It broadens our worldview and extends tolerance and empathy toward others. Ongoing learning encourages innovation and creativity. It enables us to connect ideas from various disciplines and develop novel solutions and concepts.

Learning and personal growth are fundamental to a fulfilling life. They both empower us to deal with life's challenges, contribute to our communities, and lead a purposeful and meaningful existence. By adopting the idea that it's never too late to learn something new, we Soloists can keep our minds engaged and invigorated well into the future. When we embrace learning as a lifelong avocation, we continually evolve and adapt to the ever-changing landscape of our lives and the world.

When looking for the right hobby, remember to take it slow and allow yourself the time to find what brings you joy and satisfaction. The goal isn't to become an expert overnight but to enjoy the process of learning and growing. Each new experience brings the potential for fun, fulfillment, and mental sharpness as we continue to explore and discover the activities that enhance our lives.

Overcoming Fear of the Unknown

It's natural to encounter feelings of apprehension or fear when stepping into something new. However, it's important to remember that fear should not stop us from exploring new opportunities for growth and enjoyment. Instead of allowing fear to hold us back, we can choose to approach new experiences with curiosity, openness, and a willingness to discover the unknown. Try to reframe fear as excitement and see challenges as opportunities for learning. That way, we are ready to see the joys and rewards of exploring new horizons.

Here is a consolidated approach that might be helpful. Using a journal or notepad to work through some of these tips is a good idea. Sometimes, writing things out is a very clarifying process:

Reflect on Your Values: Take some time to reflect on your priorities in life. What truly matters to you? What brings you a sense of fulfillment and meaning? Whether spending time with loved ones, pursuing creative arts, or contributing to your community, identifying your values can provide a sense of direction.

Set Intentions: Before trying out a new experience, decide what you hope to gain or learn from the experience. What do you want to achieve? How do you want to feel? Setting clear intentions can help focus your energy and attention, allowing you to approach the experience with purpose and clarity.

Listen to Your Intuition: Trust your inner voice as you start new experiences. Take some notes on how you feel in different situations, and honor your instincts. Your intuition can serve as a valuable guide, helping you make decisions that align with your values and bring you closer to your authentic self.

Practice Mindfulness: Stay present as you engage in new experiences. Take deep breaths, tune into your senses, and observe your thoughts and emotions without judgment. Mindfulness can help calm your mind, reduce anxiety, and enhance your ability to fully immerse yourself in the present moment.

Be Curious: Approach new experiences with a sense of openness. In addition to focusing on potential outcomes or expectations, allow yourself to be curious about the process itself. Adopting a curious mindset can help alleviate fear and uncertainty, allowing you to approach new experiences with a sense of adventure and anticipation.

Practice Self-Compassion: Be easy on yourself as you go into new experiences. Acknowledge any fears or doubts that arise and remind yourself that it's natural to feel uncertain when stepping outside your comfort zone. Treat yourself with kindness and understanding, knowing that growth often comes from meeting challenges and learning from them.

Stuff Gets in the Way

Sometimes, we set up roadblocks to trying new things. We do this to ourselves for several reasons. It could be fear of failure, fear of the unknown, perfectionism, past negative experiences, or external pressure or expectations. These roadblocks take the form of limiting beliefs or self-doubt that create barriers to stepping outside of our comfort zone and participating in new experiences.

Eliminating blockages requires some work. We need to focus on the obstacles just enough to challenge them without being consumed by them. The following is a list of ways to combat and overcome these roadblocks. Again, it may be constructive to write down anything important.

Limiting Beliefs: Identify negative self-talk that may hold you back from trying something new. Reflect on the thoughts or beliefs that arise when you think about starting something new. Are there any recurring patterns or narratives that keep you stuck? By shining a light on these limiting beliefs, you can begin to challenge and reframe them.

Assumptions: Take a closer look at the fears that underlie your reluctance to try something new. Are these assumptions based on past experiences, expectations of others, or self-imposed limitations? Challenge yourself to question the validity of these assumptions and consider alternative perspectives. Ask yourself whether these beliefs are serving you or holding you back from possible enjoyment.

Apprehension: Be gentle and compassionate with yourself as you work through fears. Recognize that it's natural to feel apprehensive when trying something new, and acknowledge any fears or doubts with kindness and understanding. Treat yourself with the same compassion you would offer a friend facing similar challenges, and remind yourself that taking small steps at your own pace is okay.

Look Ahead: Visualize yourself successfully overcoming roadblocks and trying something new confidently and easily. Imagine yourself stepping outside of your comfort zone and achieving your goals. Visualizing success can help reprogram your thought pattern and build confidence in navigating new experiences.

Take it Easy: Break down the process of trying something new into smaller, manageable steps. Instead of overwhelming yourself with the prospect of a big change or challenge, focus on taking small, incremental actions that move you closer to your goal. Celebrate each small victory along the way, and gradually expand your familiarity as you build confidence and momentum. Remember that growth happens outside your comfort zone, and each step you take towards trying something new brings you closer to realizing your full potential and living a life of fulfillment and purpose.

According to behavior researcher and management professor at Babson College, Keith Rollag, "People tend to approach a new skill in one of two ways: Some go in wanting to *learn* it, while others go in wanting to *master* it. It seems like a subtle difference, but it matters. The first attitude is, 'I know I don't really know how to do this. I'm going to make mistakes, but the fun here is figuring out how to do it,' while the mastering attitude is all about doing well and impressing others. Going in with the attitude of humility allows you to enjoy yourself even if you're floundering — after all, it's just part of the process. Aiming for mastery, on the other hand, sets you up for failure very quickly."

Rollag goes on to say, "That's not to say it's *all* about the journey — it's good to still have an end goal in mind. It can help, though, to think carefully about what that end goal should be, and to start with a beginner-friendly one. Maybe your new hobby is marathons, for example. Running one in under four hours is a goal, sure, but getting in shape and meeting other runners are worthy outcomes, too."

Taking the learning approach also doesn't mean going in blind. Whatever you're trying, doing a little prep work beforehand can make your first time a lot less intimidating. By taking the time to prepare mentally before a new experience, you can approach it with greater confidence and clarity. You can equip yourself with the thoughts and skills needed to begin any new experience with grace and confidence.

Support

Reach out to supportive friends, family members, or mentors who can offer encouragement, guidance, and accountability as you work through trying something new. Share your goals and aspirations with friends. They can provide constructive feedback and help you stay motivated in your new adventures.

Being a Soloist offers a unique opportunity to explore new things, take on unfamiliar challenges, and develop a sense of fulfillment and purpose. It could be pursuing long-held passions, trying out new hobbies, or any other adventures we come upon. We have time and freedom to uncover the richness and excitement that life has to offer. By remaining open-minded and curious, we can unlock a world of possibilities and create a life filled with joy. We are reaching for new horizons as an opportunity to learn, grow, and create memories that will last a lifetime.

After discovering our newfound passion, it's time to turn our attention in the next chapter to renewing body, mind, and spirit. Just as an avocation invigorates our soul, nurturing our physical, mental, and emotional well-being is essential to achieve overall health and balance in our lives. Let's explore how we can seamlessly transition from the fulfillment of pursuing our interests to revitalizing our entire being.

***

THE TAILORED SOLUTIONS

Arm yourself with the facts. Uncover the things that bring you joy.

Recognize and prioritize the essentials. An avocation can become a priority.

Sustain an optimistic outlook. Positivity enhances the learning experience and makes the process of discovering a new passion more enjoyable and fulfilling.

Engage in new activities. Never stop learning.

Cultivate new connections. The learning environment has many connections to offer.

Volunteer your time. It's very satisfying.

Look for the lessons you can learn. Find clues to your next hobby.

CHAPTER 7

RENEW YOURSELF - CREATE A JOYFUL ENVIRONMENT

The Last letter "R" on the E.M.P.O.W.E.R Path stands for Renew Yourself

In this chapter, we look at our whole environment from three distinct perspectives: physical, mental, and spiritual. We'll explore the interconnection between our personal environment and overall well-being. We will focus on how nurturing each aspect can contribute to a renewal for a more vibrant and fulfilling life. We'll look at renewing our physical surroundings by decluttering and organizing. We'll look at renewing our mental resilience by focusing on a positive mindset. Then we will take a quick look at various practices that might open our spirit. We will see practical strategies that will create more joy. There is transformative power in consciously arranging life around the best possible versions of our body (physical), mind (mental), and soul (spiritual).

Living Space

Our living spaces often hold deep emotional attachments and significance. Personal space serves as a repository of memories, identity, and comfort. Our homes have hosted many gatherings and celebrations, everyday routines and rituals. They serve as the backdrop to countless recollections that shape our sense of identity and belonging. Home is a sanctuary where we feel secure and at ease. Our living spaces provide a place to relax and be free. They are our refuge from the stresses and challenges of the outside world. The physical and emotional comfort of our home such as our cozy furnishings and personal belongings, contribute to a sense of emotional well-being and stability.

Every item in our home should add to feelings of comfort and security. If there is something that is now in the living area that holds any negative attachment, consider rehoming that piece. It doesn't matter why that thing holds tension. That's irrelevant. If you're not sure about doing this, try just removing it from your sightline for now. If you notice that you feel better without its presence, eliminate it permanently.

Our homes are a reflection of our personalities, values, and aspirations. Home is where we express ourselves creatively and authentically through interior design choices, decor, and personal touches. We fill our living spaces with elements that resonate with our sense of self and reflect our unique tastes and interests. We need to use these criteria when filling up our space. Take a moment to observe what you are living with. If anything in the space does not complement who you are, give it away. Or sell it!

We may form strong attachments to the physical location of our homes. It could be the neighborhood where we grew up, a city where we've lived for years, or a picturesque setting that holds special significance. These attachments are rooted in a sense of belonging to a community and our fond memories of the area. If you have been unhappy with your current home location, you may never have developed an attachment to that place. This could be an important indication of whether you should continue to live there or relocate. Take your time with your decisions. Just consider it until you come to a firm conclusion about your location. Love it or leave it?

Living spaces also play a role in emotional healing and stability, providing a supportive environment for processing grief, loss, or life transitions. The familiar surroundings of home offer a sense of solace during difficult times, giving us a refuge for self-care and emotional well-being. Are there too many bad memories or too much grief associated with this home? What if this place we have called home must change? What happens if all those points of connection we once had are broken? What if we realize that the current location we have called home no longer works?

There are many reasons for making a decision to relocate. A new place might align more perfectly with our current goals, priorities, and aspirations for the future. If you are still working, relocating for career advancement or job opportunities is a common reason for moving. This could involve moving to a new city or region with better job prospects, higher salaries, or opportunities for career growth.

We may choose to relocate to pursue a different lifestyle, such as moving from a bustling city to a quieter rural area or vice versa. Lifestyle factors such as outdoor activities, cultural amenities, and cost of living can influence the decision to relocate.

Family considerations might play a significant role in relocation decisions. This could involve moving closer to family members to provide support or care, reuniting with loved ones after a separation, or relocating to accommodate changes in family dynamics such as marriage, divorce, or the birth of a grandchild.

Access to quality healthcare services can be a significant factor in relocation decisions, particularly for those of us with ongoing medical needs or chronic health conditions. Relocating to a new city or region with a better climate or healthcare facilities, specialists, or medical resources may be necessary to ensure proper care and treatment.

Many Soloists choose to relocate when they retire to enjoy a different climate, lower cost of living, or access to amenities. Retirees may also relocate to be closer to family, downsize to a smaller home, or explore new opportunities for leisure and relaxation.

Downsize by Relocating

If you are weighing the benefits of relocating, you may also be considering downsizing as part of your move. Everyone can agree that it's easier to move fewer things. But parting with the accumulation of years isn't easy. The decision to move to a smaller living space will mean giving up some, if not a significant number of possessions. What to take and what to rehome is deeply personal and influenced by a combination of financial, lifestyle, health, environmental, and life stage factors. By carefully considering these factors and weighing the potential benefits and trade-offs, we can make an informed decision according to our priorities and goals for the future.

Reasons for downsizing also apply to moving to a retirement community because those accommodations will likely be smaller. Many people choose to downsize as part of a broader lifestyle shift towards simplification and minimalism. By decluttering and streamlining living spaces, we also reduce stress and enhance clarity. Downsizing pushes us to be more intentional and mindful about our possessions.

Empty nesters often find themselves with more space than they need once their children have grown and moved out. Downsizing to a smaller home or apartment can be a practical way to resize a living environment to better meet current needs and lifestyle preferences.

For Soloists with mobility issues, downsizing to a smaller, more manageable home can improve safety, accessibility, and quality of life.

Single-level living, smaller yards, and features like grab bars and wider doorways make daily activities easier and more comfortable.

Some people choose to downsize as part of their commitment to environmental sustainability. Smaller homes typically have a smaller ecological footprint, requiring fewer resources to maintain. Downsizing also may encourage more eco-friendly habits, such as reducing energy consumption and minimizing waste.

Downsize by Staying in Place

Downsizing while remaining in your current home can be a practical and effective way to simplify your living space and give yourself a fresh outlook on life. The goal would be to reduce clutter and improve functionality. Downsizing allows you to maximize your existing space by eliminating unwanted or unnecessary items and optimizing storage solutions. This can create more living space even in a smaller home. Reducing clutter and excess belongings creates a cleaner and more streamlined living space. A home containing fewer things is generally easier and faster to clean, allowing you to enjoy a simpler and more manageable lifestyle.

Tips for Downsizing in Place:

Declutter Regularly: Set a tentative schedule to declutter and purge belongings that are no longer needed or used. Make a plan. Start with one room or area at a time, sorting items into categories such as keep, donate, sell, or discard.

Prioritize Essentials: Identify essential items that you use regularly and prioritize keeping those items. Consider the functionality and utility of each item, as well as its sentimental value and importance to your daily life.

Maximize Storage: Make use of storage solutions to maximize space and minimize clutter. This could include under-bed storage, vertical shelving, closet organizers, and multi-functional furniture with built-in storage.

Digitize Paperwork: Minimize paper clutter by digitizing important documents, photographs, and files. Scan paper documents and store them digitally on a computer, external hard drive, or cloud storage service to save space and reduce physical clutter.

Downsize Furniture: Consider downsizing furniture to better fit your space and lifestyle. Choose smaller-scale furniture pieces that take up less space in your rooms.

Be Mindful of Sentimental Items: While it's important to declutter and simplify, be sure to keep a few meaningful items or mementos that bring you joy and fond memories. But avoid holding onto excessive sentimental clutter that may contribute to filling up your space.

Seek Professional Help if Needed: If parting with your things feels overwhelming or you're unsure where to start, consider getting some assistance from a professional organizer, downsizing specialist, or decluttering coach. These professionals can provide guidance, support, and practical strategies to help you simplify your living space effectively.

You can successfully downsize while remaining in your current home, creating a more organized, functional, and enjoyable living environment that better aligns with your needs and lifestyle.

Mind Space

Attitude is everything. Our mindset is a powerful tool influencing our perspectives and shaping our experiences and overall well-being. Our attitude towards life influences how we perceive and respond to challenges, setbacks, and opportunities. By cultivating a positive attitude, we can enhance our sense of empowerment, enabling us to adjust to life's ups and downs with greater optimism.

Renewing our minds for optimal mental health involves intentionally cultivating a positive and growth-oriented mindset while actively managing negative thoughts and beliefs. A positive mindset focuses on the good in every situation. Practicing gratitude and reframing negative thoughts into more constructive and optimistic perspectives are also part of a positive mindset. Positive thinking enhances mental resilience and improves overall well-being. There are three parts to maintaining a positive attitude:

1. **Self-awareness:** Pay attention to thoughts, emotions, and beliefs without judgment. By increasing awareness of our inner dialogue and underlying thinking pattern, we can cultivate a habit of positive self-talk by challenging negative thoughts and replacing them with more supportive and empowering beliefs. When faced with self-critical or pessimistic thoughts, counter them by reframing them to emphasize strengths, capabilities, and potential for growth. Working in a journal is very effective for this process.

2. **Mindfulness:** Be fully present and engaged in the moment, without judgment or attachment to past regrets or future worries. Mindfulness practices, such as meditation, deep breathing exercises, and mindful awareness, can help reduce stress, enhance emotional regulation, and promote mental clarity and focus.

Throughout the day, practice mindfulness by paying attention to thoughts, emotions, and sensations. Take opportunities to pause and check in with yourself, noticing any patterns of thinking or feeling that may affect your mood or behavior. Engage in activities mindfully, whether eating, walking, or interacting with others, by bringing your full attention to the present moment. Mindfulness enhances the richness and beauty of everyday experiences.

3. **Self-care:** Regular exercise, adequate sleep, a nutritious diet, and social connection are essential for maintaining an optimal mindset. Physical health and mental well-being are interconnected, and nurturing our bodies can have a profound impact on our mood, energy level, and cognitive function. Pay attention to your body's signals and honor its need for rest, nourishment, and movement.

As always, don't hesitate to seek professional help or support when facing challenges or experiencing mental distress. Therapists, counselors, and mental health professionals can provide valuable guidance, insight, and coping strategies to help you navigate difficult emotions and overcome obstacles. Reach out to trusted professionals or organizations in your community for assistance and support.

Spirit Space

Spirituality is a deeply personal and individual experience. Each person understands the concept of "spirit" in their own unique way. For some, spirituality may be rooted in religious beliefs and practices, providing a framework for understanding the divine and exploring questions of meaning, purpose, and transcendence. Others may find spiritual fulfillment through nature, art, or creative expression, feeling a sense of connection to something greater than themselves through the beauty and wonder of the natural world. Some may view spirituality as an inner journey of self-discovery and personal growth. They seek to cultivate qualities such as compassion, gratitude, and inner peace through specific practices. Regardless of its form, spirituality is a deeply human experience encompassing a wide range of beliefs, practices, and experiences. Exploring space for your spirit involves nurturing your inner self, connecting with your values, and developing a sense of inner peace and fulfillment. Here are some ways to explore space for your spirit:

Meditation: Practice techniques to quiet the mind, cultivate inner awareness, and foster a sense of presence and peace. Set aside time to sit quietly and focus on your connection to a sense of something greater than yourself.

Connection to Nature: Spend time outdoors to reconnect with the natural world and replenish your spirit. Take walks in the woods, sit by a tranquil lake, or spend time appreciating the beauty of the natural environment. Nature has a grounding and rejuvenating effect that can help soothe the soul and inspire feelings of awe and gratitude.

Explore Alternatives: Explore different spiritual practices and traditions that resonate with you. It could be getting in touch with your heritage. Some cultures have a distinct tradition of spirituality that you may not have explored before. Returning to cultural and spiritual roots can be a very fulfilling experience. Exploring meditation, yoga or attending religious services or spiritual gatherings may be something new. These practices can offer a sense of connection to something greater as well as provide guidance, comfort, and inspiration for life.

Reflection and Journaling: Set aside time to explore your thoughts, feelings, and experiences more deeply. Use writing as a tool for self-discovery, self-expression, and personal growth, allowing yourself to explore your hopes, fears, dreams, and aspirations in a safe and supportive space.

Mindful Movement: Yoga, tai chi, or qigong connect your body, breath, and spirit. These practices can help cultivate inner peace, balance, and harmony while promoting physical health and well-being.

Soulful Connections: Welcome others who share your values, beliefs, and interests. You will feel free to engage in deep conversations and form a spiritual community. Build supportive relationships with these people when you find them. They will give you a sense of belonging and support. You will find opportunities for growth through connection with them. They will become your "tribe".

Solo Retreats: Take time for quiet reflection to nourish your spirit and recharge your energy. A 'retreat' can be as simple as spending a day in solitude at home or immersing yourself in a retreat center where others do likewise. Or you could spend some time alone in a natural setting. Use retreat time to reflect and reconnect with yourself on a deeper level.

Making space for your spirit can create a more profound sense of inner peace, purpose, and fulfillment. Experiment with different practices and approaches to see what resonates with you and brings you closer to a sense of spiritual well-being.

Taking care of these 3 aspects of ourselves, body, mind, and spirit supports a joyful environment for our overall well-being. We cultivate vitality and energy when we prioritize physical surroundings by finding our best location. Similarly, by nurturing our mental well-being through mindfulness, self-awareness, and positive thinking, we create a peaceful and harmonious inner landscape. Finally, when we connect with our spiritual selves through our chosen practices, we tap into a deeper sense of purpose, meaning, and connection to something greater than ourselves. Together, these three sides of ourselves sustain our joyful environment characterized by balance, where every aspect of our being is nourished and renewed.

THE TAILORED SOLUTIONS

Arm yourself with the facts. Identify downsizing or relocation needs.

Recognize and prioritize the essentials. Be open to adapting your living environment and routines as needed to accommodate changes in your circumstances or priorities.

Take action only on things you can affect. Be realistic about your space.

Sustain a positive mindset. Be flexible and creative in finding solutions that enhance your quality of life.

Use your spiritual practice to restore your inner peace and harmony.

Ask for help when you need it. Therapists, organizers, and spiritual mentors can offer valuable insights on creating a joyful environment.

CHAPTER 8

THE PATH TO SERENITY

We have followed the E.M.P.O.W.E.R. PATH leading us to Grace, Joy and Dignity

The E.M.P.O.W.E.R. steppingstones on the path arrive at the place where we realize our intended result:

Grace is defined as elegance and poise in one's actions, demeanor, and interactions with others, often characterized by kindness, compassion, and humility.

Joy is a profound sense of happiness, contentment, and inner peace that arises from positive experiences, meaningful connections, and a sense of gratitude.

Dignity is the inherent worth and value of ourselves and every person, shown through self-respect, integrity, and the ability to maintain one's sense of worthiness and honor, even in challenging circumstances.

With those wonderful attributes in mind, Let's look at another real-life experience. Blogger Pamela (no last name given) writes about her mother in her blog, New Age Aging. Pamala's description of her mother has been the inspiration for this culmination of the E.M.P.O.W.E.R Path:

> "My 100-year-old mother has never been a complainer! She could have been. Her mother (my grandmother) was put in an institution when Mom was 12 years old and her dad died of pneumonia shortly afterward, leaving Mom to live with her sister. At age 17 she met my dad, got married, had the three of us, and then he left. On top of that, she lost her oldest daughter to cancer. I could go on.
>
> I asked her why she wasn't bitter. 'I have always felt loved,' Mom said.
>
> Mom was living alone at that time because of pandemic restrictions, but she maintained a positive and joyful outlook on life. Her attitude towards aging was marked by dignity and grace, and she remained active and engaged even at 100 years old, walking around her parking area daily and maintaining a close phone relationship with her remaining daughters. Her resilience and positive attitude, even in the face of adversity, serve as an inspiring example of aging with grace, joy, and dignity."

We can use the example of Pamela's mother to consciously plan to prioritize grace, joy, and dignity in our lives as our future unfolds. We always need to be aware of how we are creating our future. Part of that is to be mindful of how we are planning ahead for how our lives will be. Planning or setting intentions for the future can produce what we want. In this case, grace, joy, and dignity:

Plan on Grace: Approach life's transitions with a sense of poise and composure. By proactively addressing potential challenges and uncertainties, we can meet changes smoothly and maintain our sense of calm and integrity throughout the process.

Plan on Joy: An expectancy of a sense of security and peace of mind can contribute to building joy and contentment. Knowing that our affairs are in order and that there is a plan in place for the future can alleviate anxiety and allow us to fully savor the present moment, creating a greater sense of happiness and fulfillment.

Plan on Dignity: Planning for the future empowers us to make decisions that align with our values and priorities, preserving our confidence and autonomy. By taking proactive steps to address important matters such as healthcare, finances, and end-of-life preferences, we can ensure that our wishes are honored and our humanity is respected, even in times of vulnerability or adversity.

Getting these 3 intentions firmly in mind ensures that we will keep going in the direction of all the benefits grace, joy, and dignity bring us. When we plan to see certain things, we notice when they appear. Small things we might not have noticed before will stand out as synchronistic events that show up as happy coincidences. We might see these circumstances as evidence that we are indeed heading toward what we really want in terms of our positive future. When we notice and move into what we've planned, we are growing – enhancing our future according to our desires – more grace – more joy - more dignity. Each synchronous event builds our confidence in the future. We are continuously growing into our best possible Solo Lives.

The growth process never stops. At this point in life, we have the wisdom to know that we have a hand in the direction our growth takes. It's so much easier when we think in terms of *growth and learning* instead of seeing our identity as a rigid, unchangeable set of traits and skills.

Dr. Carol Dweck introduced the concept of a growth mindset alongside its counterpart, the fixed mindset, in her book "Mindset: The New Psychology of Success," published in 2006. The fixed mindset is characterized by the belief that qualities, skills, intelligence, personality traits, and abilities are set in stone and cannot be changed. Consequently, people with a fixed mindset tend to avoid challenges and resist learning new things. They view change as a significant source of frustration. The problem is, this mindset also hinders their progress in life. They expend considerable effort to maintain the status quo rather than adapting and evolving.

On the other hand, a growth mindset can help us change the way we see life. People with a growth mindset view challenges as opportunities, mistakes as valuable lessons, and their personality and character as ever-changing and evolving rather than static.

Remember all the important past events that have led you to how you live your life now. Take a moment to review past goals you have worked towards, your actions to achieve them, and your successes and failures along the way. You had many important insights that completely changed how you see the world. As you bring your attention back to today, you'll realize one thing: *you've been changing and growing all along*.

Embracing Change

There are two reliable skills that we have already looked at that will help us as we think about continued personal growth throughout our Solo Lives. They are an open attitude and adaptability:

An Open Attitude:
- Continue to be curious.
- Explore new interests, hobbies, and ideas.
- Stay open to new experiences.
- Challenge assumptions and be open to considering alternative viewpoints.
- Embrace diversity.

Adaptability:
- View setbacks and mistakes as opportunities for learning.

- Follow the creative process in all its ups and downs.

- Acknowledge that change is essential for personal growth.

- Recognize and accept the inevitability of change.

Embracing Relationships

Our evolution into a confident, ongoing future includes others in all the many relationships we have formed along the way. We must acknowledge that those people are also changing and growing just as we are. Some of our relationships may grow deeper, and some may diminish. All relationships are valuable, and just because one or two may not seem as strong at the moment, that doesn't mean the connection will never come back better and stronger than ever. We can't control the actions of others, but we can control our side of the friendship. Staying connected to friends or family members while navigating our own growth and change requires intentional effort and flexibility.

Show empathy and understanding towards your friend's growth and changes, recognizing that everyone evolves over time and may have different needs, priorities, or perspectives that might not be in sync with our own. As we have discussed in Chapter 5, offer unconditional support and encouragement, celebrate successes, and comfort during challenges or setbacks. Respect boundaries, autonomy, and individuality, allowing space for personal growth and self-discovery while maintaining a strong foundation of trust and mutual respect.

Embracing Simplicity

As with other aspects of life, we are individuals and uniquely choose what is important to us. With that in mind, it feels good to strip away the complexities of modern life and define our own version of simplicity. Take some time to decide what truly matters. The world is filled with constant distractions and demands. Embracing simplicity clarifies the chaos outside of us and gives us inner peace.

We can simplify our schedules in the same way we intentionally chose to declutter our physical spaces. A great goal would be to streamline our lives to create room for what brings us joy and fulfillment. Simplicity frees us from consumerism, comparison, and overstimulation. This helps us appreciate life's simple pleasures and become more grateful in the present moment. When we create our own version of simplicity, we discover new possibilities and richness in life.

Embracing the Future

The following is a reflection from Gayle Kirschenbaum. She is an Emmy-winning filmmaker, photographer, writer, coach and speaker. Her film LOOK AT US NOW, MOTHER! Premiered on Netflix and has been credited with transforming lives. To learn more about Gayle's work, visit GayleKirschenbaum.com.

> "...When my brother was dying of cancer, he said, "I want you to know I'm very jealous of you." I was sure he was saying this because I was healthy, and he was not. I later asked him why and was shocked by his response. 'Because you've lived your life as a free spirit,' he told me. It was only then that I learned that this very successful man, who

built a law firm, owned a big house and luxury cars, and had children and grandchildren often felt 'trapped.' I sometimes wonder if I made a mistake by living my life alone. Am I going to pay for it as I age? Right now, at this age and stage, with the choices I have made, I am doing quite well. As I've entered my golden years, I'm joining photography, writing and meditation groups. I'm finding friends who share my athletic interests in tennis, biking and sailing. I have no regrets. I am grateful for what I've accomplished, and for the lives that have been changed by the films I've made. I still have my health, and my drive and ability to create. Instead of having children to guide to discover their individual passions and pursuits, I did succeed at guiding myself. If my soulmate gets his GPS to finally work and finds me, my arms and heart will be open to receive him. I pray he is in good health and not in debt. As for missing out on cuddling kids? While I do love my time with my brothers' children and grandchildren, it's nice to go home to my peaceful and undisturbed home. As I continue feeding my mind, body and spirit, and my health and wits stay strong, I have a lot more living to do. If I follow my mother's longevity path, this gives me 30 more years to age with finesse and continue to create art that changes lives."

Here, Gayle reminds us that being a Soloist is a perfectly acceptable way to live. Some people envy us for our freedom. She is a great example of living an enjoyable Solo Life. Remember that we are brimming with untapped potential for a vibrant and fulfilling life. We can face age-related challenges with courage, celebrate our accomplishments, and believe in our capacity to create a confident Solo Future.

As we come to the end of our journey on the E.M.P.O.W.E.R. Path, let's reflect on the wisdom we've gained. Or perhaps we've had this wisdom all along and we bring it to mind again as we remember to step into our power. While the future may hold uncertainties and challenges, we have equipped ourselves with ideas and strategies to live resiliently. We have seen how creating an expectancy of grace, joy, and dignity can bring these qualities into our lives. Take a moment to savor the richness of life experience. With each step forward from this point on, may we continue to find serenity amid life's complexities, and may our journey be filled with many wonderful moments of contentment and fulfillment.

***

THE TAILORED SOLUTIONS

Arm yourself with the facts. Pay attention to occurrences that align with your intentions for grace, joy, and dignity. Recognize these moments as evidence that you're moving toward your desired future.

Maintain social connections. Do everything you can to keep friendships strong.

Recognize and prioritize the essentials. Proactively address potential challenges and uncertainties. Maintain your sense of calm and integrity throughout the process.

Sustain an optimistic outlook. Adopt a growth mindset and view change as a natural part of life.

Take action only on things you can affect. Create an expectancy of the future you desire.

Practice self-care. Empower yourself to make decisions that align with your values while preserving your autonomy.

Look for the lessons you can learn. View challenges as opportunities for personal development and cultivate flexibility, resilience, and adaptability in navigating life's ups and downs.

CONCLUSION

We extend our heartfelt gratitude to you, our fellow Soloists, for embarking on this empowering path with us. Through the pages of this book, we've navigated the complexities of aging solo, exploring the depths of our resilience and celebrating the unique qualities that define us. Together, we've uncovered the wisdom to embrace our future years with confidence and autonomy.

As you close this book, we hope you carry with you a renewed sense of self and well-being. May you walk forward into the next chapter of your life, knowing that age does not define us but enriches the tapestry of our experiences.

It's time for us to flourish in Solo Living, to revel in the freedom and autonomy that comes with embracing our individual paths. May we move confidently into a future filled with boundless opportunities for growth, connection, and renewal. May your days ahead be filled with moments of joy, purpose, and fulfillment, as you continue to live your best possible Solo Life.

Remember, you are not alone on this journey. Together, we stand as a community of strong, resilient Soloists, ready to support and uplift one another as we navigate the adventures that lie ahead. You can do this by leaving a review for this book for other to find. Thank you for being a part of this E.M.P.O.W.E.R. Path and may your future be filled with endless possibilities and abundant blessings.

Reach Out and Make a Difference!

Your insights are invaluable. By sharing your thoughts, you can guide others seeking support in their Solo Aging journey.

Your review matters. It's a guiding light for those navigating the complexities of Aging Solo. Together, let's illuminate the path forward for others.

Click on the book image or use the link below to leave a review.

https://www.amazon.com/review/create-review/?ie=UTF8&channel=glance-detail&asin=B0D3FQC78K

Be sure to check out our other books at https://daisy-publishing.com/

REFERENCES

References

4 Steps to Preparing finances for Divorce | Wells Fargo. (n.d.). https://www.wellsfargo.com/financial-health/life-events/divorce-finances/

4 steps to walk away from loneliness | McLean Hospital. (2023, July 13). https://www.mcleanhospital.org/essential/loneliness

30 Lessons for Living: Tried and True Advice from the Wisest Americans: Pillemer Ph.D., Karl: 9780452298484: Amazon.com: Books. (n.d.). https://www.amazon.com/30-Lessons-Living-Advice-Americans/dp/0452298482

A disproportionate number of Black women are "kinless" as they age. Advocates say they deserve a social safety net, too. (2023, December 26). Fortune Well. https://fortune.com/well/article/kinless-older-black-women-social-legal-benefits/

Activities that can boost a senior's confidence | Columbia Pacific Communities. (2022, September 6). Columbia Pacific Communities. https://www.columbiacommunities.in/article/activities-that-can-boost-a

-seniors-confidence-useful-insights-by-one-of-the-senior-living-communities-for-nris/

Adcox, S. (2022, June 6). *What to know about Existential dread*. WebMD. https://www.webmd.com/mental-health/what-to-know-existential-dread

Admin. (2019, October 29). *5 Benefits of downsizing for Seniors*. Concordia Life Plan Community. https://concordiaseniorliving.com/blog/5-benefits-of-downsizing-for-seniors/

Admin. (2023a, April 11). *Achieving wellness: top strategies for nurturing a healthy body and why it matters – The Yale Wave*. https://campuspress.yale.edu/wave/achieving-wellness-top-strategies-for-nurturing-a-healthy-body-and-why-it-matters/

Admin. (2023b, July 15). *Retirees' Wish List: Unveiling the ideal lifestyle and experiences Retirees seek – Titan Strongman*. https://titanostrongman.com/retirees-wish-list-unveiling-the-ideal-lifestyle-and-experiences-retirees-seek/

aging. (2022, November 2). Psychology Today. https://www.psychologytoday.com/us/basics/aging

Alasagas, A. (2022, April 28). *Younger women shop more, but older women spend more – study*. Marketing Mag. https://www.marketingmag.com.au/tech-data/younger-women-shop-older-women-spend-study/

Alder, B. (2016, March 29). *6 steps to eliminate roadblocks — Burke Alder - entrepreneur - marketing leader - adventurer*. Burke Alder - Entrepreneur - Marketing Leader - Adventurer. https://www.burkealder.com/leadership/six-steps-to-eliminate-roadblocks

*Amazon.com: The Social Cure: Identity, Health and Well-Being: 9781848720213: Jetten, Jolanda, Haslam, Catherine, Haslam, Alexander

S.: Books. (n.d.). https://www.amazon.com/Social-Cure-Identity-Healh-Well-Being/dp/1848720211

Ardencoaching. (2023, December 25). How to get comfortable in uncomfortable settings. *Arden Coaching*. https://ardencoaching.com/get-comfortable-uncomfortable-settings/

Bello, C. (2018, March 1). The power of connecting with like-minded individuals. *Chris Bello*. https://chrisbello.com/the-power-of-connecting-with-like-minded-individuals/

Bisous, B. (2023, June 27). Exploring different types of spirituality: from Buddhism to shamanism. *website*. https://www.bijoubisous.com/single-post/exploring-different-types-of-spirituality-from-buddhism-to-shamanism

Broker, C. H.-. (2023, May 30). Want to budget and get results? *mortgageedgequinte*. https://www.mortgageedgequinte.com/post/want-to-budget-and-get-results

Buckner Retirement Services. (2023, August 15). *How finding new hobbies can help seniors*. https://bucknerretirement.org/blog/how-finding-new-hobbies-can-help-seniors/

Cafasso, J. (2023, February 20). *How fear of a diagnosis affects people at risk of Alzheimer's disease*. Healthline. https://www.healthline.com/health/alzheimers/fearing-alzheimers-diagnosis

CDS, E. C. K. C., & CDS, E. C. K. C. (2024, February 16). *Senior Safety advice*. Senior Safety Advice. https://seniorsafetyadvice.com/aging-is-a-privilege/

Center for Healthy Aging Research. (2024, February 16). College of Health. https://health.oregonstate.edu/healthy-aging

Change, I. (2020, December 11). *How to embrace change in your life*. Intelligent Change. https://www.intelligentchange.com/blogs/read/how-to-embrace-change-in-your-life

Chapter tOO LLC - Business Optimization Firm. (n.d.). *resilience Archives*. Chapter tOO Talent and Business Consulting. https://chaptertoo.com/tag/resilience/

Cheyette, B. C. M. a. S., MD. (2021, November 23). One simple habit can build a lifetime of motivation. *Psychology Today*. https://www.psychologytoday.com/us/blog/1-2-3-adhd/202111/why-its-important-celebrate-small-successes

Chronic illness. (2024, January 24). Psychology Today. https://www.psychologytoday.com/us/basics/chronic-illness

Cirino, E. (2019, April 3). *How to Relax: Tips for chilling out*. Healthline. https://www.healthline.com/health/stress/how-to-relax

Clinic, C. F. M. (2022, November 21). *Finding the right primary care clinic*. Your Family Medical Clinic. https://yourfamilymedicalclinic.com/blog/finding-the-right-primary-care-clinic/

Cognitive Behavioral therapy. (2024, January 24). Psychology Today. https://www.psychologytoday.com/us/basics/cognitive-behavioral-therapy

Communities - where you live matters. (n.d.). Where You Live Matters. https://www.whereyoulivematters.org/find-a-community/

Communities, A. a. I. a. L. (2023, November 16). 7 Steps To Overcome the Fear of Change | CT & MA Assisted Living Conversations | The Arbors. *The Arbors & The Ivy Assisted Living*. https://arborsassistedliving.com/7-steps-to-overcoming-fear-of-change/

Corp, N. C. S. T. A., Corp, N. C. S. T. A., & Corp, N. C. S. T. A. (2023, July 18). *If you're feeling hopeless about being single, ditch these 16 habits now | #datingscams | #lovescams | #datingscams | #love | #relationships |*

#scams | #pof | #match.com | #dating. National Cyber Security Consulting - National Cyber Security. https://nationalcybersecurity.com/if-youre-feeling-hopeless-about-being-single-ditch-these-16-habits-now-datingscams-lovescams-datingscams-love-relationships-scams-pof-match-com-dating/

Cwrn-Admin. (2023, March 24). *5 ways to improve workplace success*. Cenla Work Ready Network. https://www.cenlaworkready.org/blog/5-ways-to-improve-workplace-success/

Deneme Bonusu. (2024, April 4). *Deneme bonusu veren siteler 2024 - Deneme bonusu 2024*. https://youbetterself.com/

Dennis, H., & Gqlshare. (2023, January 29). How to stay open to new experiences and passions as you age. *Daily News*. https://www.dailynews.com/2023/01/29/how-to-stay-open-to-new-experiences-and-passions-as-you-age/

Deron, B. (2024, February 29). 18 best gifts for older women to shop now. *Us Weekly*. https://www.usmagazine.com/shop-with-us/news/best-gifts-for-older-women/

Dev, H. (2020, December 4). *What you need to know about social and emotional changes in old age*. Stowell Associates. https://stowellassociates.com/what-are-the-emotional-needs-of-the-elderly/

Digital, T. N. (2020, November 10). Include these 5 fruits in your winter diet to boost your immunity. *Times Now*. https://www.timesnownews.com/health/article/include-these-5-fruits-in-your-winter-diet-to-boost-your-immunity/677181

Dolan, M. (2020, October 12). *Women over age 60 who inspire wellness, living your best life*. EverydayHealth.com. https://www.everydayhealth.com/womens-health/women-over-age-who-inspire-wellness-healthy-aging/

Don't let the fear of destitution define your money habits. (2022, July 19). Fulcrum Financial Group. https://fulcrumfinancialgroup.com/blog/destitution

Emamzadeh, A. (2021, July 5). A new review identifies 8 common factors that contribute to identity change. *Psychology Today.* https://www.psychologytoday.com/us/blog/finding-new-home/202107/how-identity-change-happens

Emotional intelligence. (2024, February 27). Psychology Today. https://www.psychologytoday.com/us/basics/emotional-intelligence

Experts told: You can reduce the risk of dementia by 40%, for this start these three things from now. (2023, May 20). Newscrab. https://www.newscrab.com/lifestyle/experts-told-you-can-reduce-the-risk-of-dementia-by-40-for/cid10977360.htm

Exploring the mental health impact of aging women. (n.d.). Community Connection | Baylor University. https://communityconnection.web.baylor.edu/news/story/2020/exploring-mental-health-impact-aging-women

Finding inner peace in the chaos of life: Practical tips and techniques. (2024, March 14). A2ZOFLIFE. https://a2zoflife.com/insights/finding-inner-peace-in-the-chaos-of-life-practical-tips-and-techniques

Five tips for choosing a new primary care physician | Blue Cross Blue Shield. (n.d.). https://www.bcbs.com/the-health-of-america/articles/five-tips-choosing-new-primary-care-physician

Friendship Lessons from Mahabharat. (2023, May 27). Brain Power Study. https://brainpowerstudy.com/blog/brain-power-s-blogs-1/friendship-lessons-from-mahabharat-8

Graham Estate Planning. (2023, April 7). *Healthcare directives | Graham Estate Planning.* Graham Estate

Planning | Plan for Tomorrow, Prepare for the Future. https://grahamestateplanning.com/services/healthcare-directives/

Gupta, S. (2023, May 30). *Why identity matters and how it shapes us.* Verywell Mind. https://www.verywellmind.com/why-identity-matters-and-how-it-shapes-us-7504546

Heights, H. H. (2023, March 21). 8 Benefits of Hobbies for Seniors - Havenwood Heritage Heights. *Havenwood Heritage Heights.* https://hhhinfo.com/blog/8-benefits-of-hobbies-for-seniors/

Holt-Lunstad, J., Smith, T. B., & Layton, J. B. (2010). Social Relationships and Mortality Risk: A Meta-analytic review. *PLoS Medicine, 7*(7), e1000316. https://doi.org/10.1371/journal.pmed.1000316

How does inflation affect your credit card debt? Here's what you need to know. (n.d.). https://www.gauss.money/inflations_impact_on_credit_card_debt

How to cope when your looks fade - HealthGuidance.org. (n.d.). https://www.healthguidance.org/entry/18032/1/how-to-cope-when-your-looks-fade.html

Irving, J. (2023, August 1). The benefits of independent living: thriving in a supportive and active environment. *Generations, LLC.* https://www.generationsllc.com/resources/blog/benefits-independent-living-supportive-active-environment/

Jackson, S., & Jackson, S. (2023, July 21). Building strong family bonds « Moms don't have time to. *Moms Don't Have Time To « The Modern Woman's Guide to Empowered Living.* https://www.momsdonthavetimeto.net/family-bonds/building-strong-family-bonds/

Jackson-McCulloch, J. (2023, September 20). *Alone but not lonely: Tips for solo aging.* Elder Advisory Group.

https://www.elderadvisorygroup.com/alone-but-not-lonely-tips-for-solo-aging/

Jasminechinnaphan. (2024, January 4). *Finding your passion when you're over 55*. True Connection Communities. https://www.trueconnectioncommunities.com/senior-living-blog/discovering-your-passion-over-55-communities/

Kallal, L. (2015, May 21). *A Simple Process to Turn Fear into Power*. Tiny Buddha. https://tinybuddha.com/blog/a-simple-process-to-turn-fear-into-power/

Kapil, R. (2020, August 18). *Where to seek professional mental health support - Mental health First Aid*. Mental Health First Aid. https://www.mentalhealthfirstaid.org/2020/08/where-to-seek-professional-mental-health-support/

Kirschenbaum, G. (2021, November 2). *What it's Like to Still Be Single at Age 66*. The Ethel. https://www.aarpethel.com/relationships/what-its-like-to-still-be-single-at-age-66

Kirschenbaum, G. (2022, November 28). *Why I have no regrets about aging solo with no kids*. The Ethel. https://www.aarpethel.com/relationships/why-i-have-no-regrets-about-aging-solo-with-no-kids

Kyröläinen, A., Gillett, J., Karabin, M., Sonnadara, R., & Kuperman, V. (n.d.). *Cognitive and social well-being in older adulthood: The CoSoWELL corpus of written life stories*. Behavior Research Methods. https://doi.org/10.3758/s13428-022-01926-0

Lcsw, B. C. P. (2023, August 11). How to overcome health anxiety with cognitive behavioral therapy. *Psychology Today*. https://www.psychologytoday.com/us/blog/managing-health-anxiety/202308/the-vicious-cycle-of-health-anxiety

Lcsw, K. K. M. (2021, April 2). *Older people grieve differently*. Center for Grief and Trauma Therapy. https://www.centerforgrieftherapy.com/older-people-grieve-differently/

Lcsw, M. D. (2021, August 30). *Self-Esteem in Seniors: Activities to Boost confidence*. Blue Moon Senior Counseling. https://bluemoonseniorcounseling.com/self-esteem-in-seniors-activities-to-boost-confidence/

Lcsw, M. D. (2022, October 12). *The Effects of aging on Identity - Blue Moon Senior Counseling*. Blue Moon Senior Counseling. https://bluemoonseniorcounseling.com/the-effects-of-aging-on-identity/

LearnVest. (2021, January 7). 6 Common financial fears -- and how to conquer them. *Forbes*. https://www.forbes.com/sites/learnvest/2014/10/02/6-common-financial-fears-and-how-to-conquer-them/?sh=66687e494831

Life expectancy in the United States. (2006). In *CRS Reports*. https://www.everycrsreport.com/reports/RL32792.html

LifeHack. (2024, January 19). *LifeHack - More time. more action. more meaning*. Lifehack. https://www.lifehack.org/

Lifespark, & Lifespark. (2023, April 18). How social connections Keep Seniors healthy | Shakopee. *All Saints Senior Living - All Saints Senior Living*. https://allsaintsseniorliving.com/how-social-connections-keep-seniors-healthy/

Lifestyle and chronic pain. (2022). In *MDPI eBooks*. https://doi.org/10.3390/books978-3-0365-3577-7

Living, A. S. S. (n.d.). *9 Activities for Seniors that Can Improve Self-Confidence | All Seasons Senior Living*. https://allseasonsseniorliving.com/9-activities-for-seniors-that-can-improve-self-confidence/

Living well through crisis. (n.d.). Cornell College of Human Ecology. https://www.human.cornell.edu/spotlights/living-well-through-crisis

Lopatin, A. (2023, February 21). *Make New Friends and Keep the Old: How to nurture existing relationships and confidently form new ones.* Dr. Sharon Saline. https://drsharonsaline.com/2021/12/19/make-new-friends-and-keep-the-old-how-to-nurture-existing-relationships-and-confidently-form-new-ones/

MacLeod, S., Musich, S., Hawkins, K., Alsgaard, K., & Wicker, E. (2016). The impact of resilience among older adults. *Geriatric Nursing, 37*(4), 266–272. https://doi.org/10.1016/j.gerinurse.2016.02.014

Madison. (2023, January 9). Downsizing for Seniors: 10 helpful tips – MeetCaregivers. *MeetCaregivers*. https://meetcaregivers.com/downsizing-for-seniors-helpful-tips/

Manning, M. (2019a, August 20). *7 Positive ways to overcome your fear of Death.* Sixty and Me. https://sixtyandme.com/6-positive-ways-to-reduce-your-fear-of-death-sixty/

Manning, M. (2019b, September 8). *Addressing the top 6 fears of women over 60.* Sixty and Me. https://sixtyandme.com/the-top-6-fears-of-women-over-60/#:~:text=Fear%20of%20Death,life%2C%20as%20we%20know%20it

Marriage. (2024, February 16). Psychology Today. https://www.psychologytoday.com/us/basics/marriage

Mazzo, L. (2023, December 15). 3 Ways to take care of your mental health as you get older. *SELF*. https://www.self.com/story/aging-mental-health-tips

McCauley, M. C. (2019, August 19). Retirement communities, performing groups, provide arts outreach to seniors. *Baltimore Sun*. https://www.baltimoresun.com/2014/05/03/retirement-communities-performing-groups-provide-arts-outreach-to-seniors/

McCoy, B. (2021, December 20). How your brain copes with grief, and why it takes time to heal. *NPR*. https://www.npr.org/sections/health-shots/2021/12/20/1056741090/grief-loss-holiday-brain-healing

McCracken, A. (2022, March 4). How to Love Yourself: 6 Therapist-Backed Tips for Practicing Self-Love and Self-Acceptance. *SELF*. https://www.self.com/story/how-to-love-yourself

Medicare in Haines City, FL. (2023, October 3). 1st Class Insurance Services Agency. https://www.1stclassinsurance.com/coverage/medicare/

Meyer, C. (2023, December 26). *7 Tips for thriving When Living Alone After 60*. SWM. https://secondwindmovement.com/living-alone-after-60/

Mindset – suiprogressio.com. (2023, June 23). https://suiprogressio.com/75/mindset/

Msj, J. C. (2018, December 10). *The No BS Guide to Protecting your Emotional space*. Healthline. https://www.healthline.com/health/mental-health/set-boundaries

Mt. (2020, August 13). *10 people who found big success later in life*. VANTAGE Aging. https://vantageaging.org/blog/success-later-in-life/

Mt. (2022, October 24). *9 Benefits of volunteering for older adults*. VANTAGE Aging. https://vantageaging.org/blog/benefits-older-adults-gain-volunteering/

Muir, B. (2023, July 4). *Avoiding family feuds: Why you need estate planning lawyers - California beat*. California Beat. https://www.californiabeat.org/avoiding-family-feuds/

Murthy, V. H. (2023). *Our Epidemic of Loneliness and Isolation: The U.S. Surgeon General's Advisory on the Healing Effects of Social Connection and Community*. https://www.hhs.gov/sites/default/files/surgeon-general-social-connection-advisory.pdf

Neto Financial Group. (2024, March 8). *Financial & Accounting Advisors Nashville, Brentwood TN | Neto Financial*. Neto Financial Group - Financial Services for Small Business Owners and Working Professionals. https://netofinancial.com/

Nourishing Recovery: The Transformative Effects of a wholesome Diet on life After Cancer Treatment | Gifts of Hope. (2023, August 28). https://giftsofhopetx.org/2023/08/28/nourishing-recovery-the-transformative-effects-of-a-wholesome-diet-on-life-after-cancer-treatment/

Nutrition as We Age: Healthy Eating with the Dietary Guidelines - News & Events | health.gov. (n.d.). https://health.gov/news/202107/nutrition-we-age-healthy-eating-dietary-guidelines

O'Brien, J., & O'Brien, J. (2023, June 30). Moving House: Tips and tricks for solo movers. *House Integrals*. https://houseintegrals.com/moving-house-tips-and-tricks-for-solo-movers/

Omnia Health. (2023, July 24). *How To Find The Doctor That’s Right For You*. https://omniahealthco.com/how-to-find-the-doctor-thats-right-for-you/

Oneclickinfo. (2023, July 17). *Your guide to hobbies and passions in retirement | Senior Home Care*. A Better Way in Homecare. https://abetterwayinhomecare.com/how-find-passions-retirement.html

O'Neill, M. (2023, January 18). Jane Fonda's tip for making real friends as you get older makes so much sense. *SELF*. https://www.self.com/story/jane-fonda-adult-friendship-tip

Onovae, A. K., & Onovae, A. K. (2023, September 18). *Navigating personal finances in uncertain times*. CorrectNG. https://www.correctng.com/navigating-personal-finances-in-uncertain-times-strategies-for-stability/

Outreach. (2021, October 5). *The importance of physical health for better mental health.* Sage Neuroscience Center. https://sageclinic.org/blog/healthy-body-mental-health/

Petersen, A. (2021, August 31). *Why single seniors say yes to senior living | The Ridge.* The Ridge Senior Living. https://theridgeseniorliving.com/blog/why-single-seniors-thrive-in-senior-living-communities/

Phillips-Waller, S. (2023, August 22). *15 Truths to help you Overcome your fear of being judged.* A Conscious Rethink. https://www.aconsciousrethink.com/12596/fear-of-being-judged/

Primary Care - Murray Medical & Wellness Centers. (2023, January 16). Murray Medical & Wellness Centers. https://murraymed.com/primary-care/

Puzianowska-Kuźnicka, M., Owczarz, M., Wieczorowska-Tobis, K., Nadrowski, P., Chudek, J., Ślusarczyk, P., Skalska, A., Jonas, M., Franek, E., & Mossakowska, M. (2016). Interleukin-6 and C-reactive protein, successful aging, and mortality: the PolSenior study. *Immunity & Ageing, 13*(1). https://doi.org/10.1186/s12979-016-0076-x

Rampton, J. (2023, May 19). 8 Legitimate Retirement Fears & How to Overcome your real money fear. *Medium.* https://medium.com/@johnrampton/8-legitimate-retirement-fears-how-to-overcome-your-real-money-fear-b4681181b9ae

Raypole, C. (2024, February 7). *Tips for building a stronger relationship.* Healthline. https://www.healthline.com/health/healthy-relationship

Reilly, K. (2022, November 13). How to cope with grief when it feels overwhelming. *Vox.* https://www.vox.com/even-better/23445017/cumulative-grief-loss-overwhelming-cope-mental-health

Resilience. (n.d.). https://www.apa.org. https://www.apa.org/topics/resilience

Richards, L. (2022, March 18). *What is positive self-talk?* https://www.medicalnewstoday.com/articles/positive-self-talk

Rodriguez, D. (2021, October 6). *5 tips for older adults to rediscover your passions – Tapestry Senior.* https://www.tapestrysenior.com/2021/10/06/5-tips-for-older-adults-to-rediscover-your-passions/

Romm, C. (2018, January 9). How to conquer your fear of trying new things. *The Cut.* https://www.thecut.com/article/how-to-conquer-your-fear-of-trying-new-things.html

Roy, E. (2024, April 9). *Volunteering.* Montreal West. https://montreal-west.ca/en/resident-services/senior-services/volunteering/

Saravesi, P. (2016, June 30). *Overcoming the Challenges of Eating Solo - Senior Care Advice & Caregiver Support.* Senior Care Advice & Caregiver Support. https://seniorcareadvice.com/health-well-being/health-safety/overcoming-the-challenges-of-eating-solo.htm

Scott, E., PhD. (2023, December 5). How to cope with loneliness. *Verywell Mind.* https://www.verywellmind.com/how-to-cope-with-loneliness-3144939

Seegert, L. (2018, July 9). *Bag Lady Syndrome: the fear of dying broke and alone.* Silver Century Foundation. https://www.silvercentury.org/2017/03/losing-sleep-for-fear-of-becoming-a-bag-lady/

Self-Esteem. (2024, January 24). Psychology Today. https://www.psychologytoday.com/us/basics/self-esteem

Self-Perceptions and Behavior of Older People living Alone - PMC (nih.gov). (n.d.). Self-Perceptions and Behavior of Older People Living Alone - PMC (nih.gov).

Senior Services of America. (2023, November 3). *10 Tips for downsizing for Seniors - Senior Services of America.* https://seniorservicesofamerica.com/blog/10-tips-for-downsizing-for-seniors/

Senior Women | Anxiety and Depression Association of America, ADAA. (n.d.). https://adaa.org/find-help-for/women/senior-women

Silva, N. M. L. E., Gonçalves, R. A., Pascoal, T. A., Lima-Filho, R. A., De Paula França Resende, E., Vieira, E., Teixeira, A. L., De Souza, L. C., Peny, J. A., Fortuna, J. T., Furigo, I. C., Hashiguchi, D., Miya-Coreixas, V. S., Clarke, J. R., Abisambra, J. F., Longo, B. M., Donato, J., Fraser, P. E., Rosa-Neto, P., . . . De Felice, F. G. (2021). Pro-inflammatory interleukin-6 signaling links cognitive impairments and peripheral metabolic alterations in Alzheimer's disease. *Translational Psychiatry, 11*(1). https://doi.org/10.1038/s41398-021-01349-z

Social Security history. (n.d.). https://www.ssa.gov/history/reports/ces/cesbookc7.html

Stacy. (2022, August 22). *How to live on a fixed income successfully.* Six Dollar Family. https://sixdollarfamily.com/how-to-live-on-a-fixed-income-successfully

Staff, C. (2024, January 31). *What are interpersonal skills? and how to strengthen them.* Coursera. https://www.coursera.org/articles/interpersonal-skills

Staff, M. (2024, February 21). *How to practice gratitude.* Mindful. https://www.mindful.org/an-introduction-to-mindful-gratitude/

Stefanacci, R. G. (2024, April 10). *Changes in the body with aging.* MSD Manual Consumer Version. https://www.msdmanuals.com/home/older-people%E2%80%99s-health-issues/the-aging-body/changes-in-the-body-with-aging

Strategies, I. (2024, January 28). *The positive impact of resilience in older adults - where you live matters.* Where You Live Matters. https://www.whereyoulivematters.org/resources/resilience-and-aging/

Strauman, T. J., & Higgins, E. T. (1987). Automatic activation of self-discrepancies and emotional syndromes: When cognitive structures influence affect. *Journal of Personality and Social Psychology, 53*(6), 1004–1014. https://doi.org/10.1037/0022-3514.53.6.1004

Tannenbaum, J., & Tannenbaum, J. (2021, December 5). What are Creative Outlets & Why Do They Matter? - Julia Tannenbaum. *Julia Tannenbaum - Author & Activist*. https://thenaturalnovelist.com/what-are-creative-outlets-and-why-they-matter/

Tg. (2022, November 28). *Consider a broker when applying for Medicare*. Senior Learning Institute St. Louis. https://seniorlearninginstitute.com/blog/consider-a-broker-when-applying-for-medicare/

The National Council on Aging. (n.d.). https://www.ncoa.org/article/how-older-adults-can-get-help-paying-for-housing

The truth about beauty. (n.d.). Psychology Today. https://www.psychologytoday.com/us/articles/201011/the-truth-about-beauty

Theujjwal. (2023, June 3). Exam Anxiety and Stress Management: Tips for a calm and Confident Mindset - The Ujjwal. *The Ujjwal*. https://www.theujjwal.in/exam-anxiety-and-stress-management-tips-for-a-calm-and-confident-mindset/

Thich, B. (2024, April 13). *What is the 50/30/20 Rule Budget & How to Use it? - FinSavvy Panda*. FinSavvy Panda. https://www.finsavvypanda.com/50-30-20-rule-budget/

Todays Seniors. (2023, April 14). *Todays seniors*. https://www.todaysseniors.com/

"True cost of aging" index shows many U.S. seniors can't afford basic necessities. (2022, July 27). *CBS News*.

https://www.cbsnews.com/news/retirement-many-seniors-cant-afford-basic-necessities/

Twenge, J. M. (2019). More time on technology, Less happiness? Associations between Digital-Media Use and Psychological Well-Being. *Current Directions in Psychological Science, 28*(4), 372–379. https://doi.org/10.1177/0963721419838244

Understanding Grief and Loss | McLean Hospital. (2023, October 20). https://www.mcleanhospital.org/essential/grief

Upham, B. (2022, April 12). *Help ease chronic pain with integrative medicine.* EverydayHealth.com. https://www.everydayhealth.com/wellness/united-states-of-stress/manage-stress-with-integrative-medicine/

US Census Bureau. (2023a, November 1). *All the Single Ladies: Washington, D.C., Has the Highest Ratio of Unmarried Women to Unmarried Men.* Census.gov. https://www.census.gov/library/stories/2023/09/unmarried-women-men.html

US Census Bureau. (2023b, November 2). *Unmarried and Single Americans Week: September 17-23, 2023.* Census.gov. https://www.census.gov/newsroom/stories/unmarried-single-americans-week.html

Villa-Forte, A. (2022, September 12). *Effects of aging on the musculoskeletal system.* MSD Manual Consumer Version. https://www.msdmanuals.com/home/bone,-joint,-and-muscle-disorders/biology-of-the-musculoskeletal-system/effects-of-aging-on-the-musculoskeletal-system

Vosberg, M. M. (2022, May 26). *Downsizing benefits for the 60-Something Woman: Are you ready to explore them?* Sixty and Me. https://sixtyandme.com/downsizing-benefits-for-the-60-something-woman-are-you-ready-to-explore-them/

Walker, H. (2023, April 6). *National Volunteer Month: Giving Back and Making a difference.* Dream Maker Pins. https://dreammakerpins.com/blogs/welcome-blog/national-volunteer-month

Wellness, T. (2022, December 19). *Coping up with long distance family relationships.* The Wellness Corner. https://www.thewellnesscorner.com/blog/long-distance-family-relationships

What are the benefits of older adults engaging in community service? (2023, September 24). www.linkedin.com. https://www.linkedin.com/advice/0/what-benefits-older-adults-engaging-community-service

What is a yogi? Understanding the ancient practice of yoga. (n.d.). Aura. https://www.aurahealth.io/blog/what-is-a-yogi-understanding-the-ancient-practice-of-yoga

Whelchel, S. (2023, March 5). A few simple thoughts on having a comfortable fixed income retirement. *CCRH Home Retirement.* https://www.ccrh.net/post/a-few-simple-thoughts-on-having-a-comfortable-fixed-income-retirement

'Who am I?' How to find your sense of self. (2020, June 18). Healthline. https://www.healthline.com/health/sense-of-self#importance

Williams, L. (2013, October 29). *Don't Just Do Something; Sit There! - Leadershift Consulting | Leslie Williams | Leading with Grit & Grace.* Leadershift Consulting | Leslie Williams | Leading With Grit & Grace. https://leadershift.net/dont-just-do-something-sit-there/

Williams, L. (2023, June 12). *Cumulative Grief aka Grief Overload - What's Your Grief.* Whats Your Grief. https://whatsyourgrief.com/cumulative-grief-aka-grief-overload/

Wu, J., PhD. (2020, September 8). You might be surprised by the factors that influence our attitudes toward death. *Psychology Today.*

https://www.psychologytoday.com/us/blog/the-savvy-psychologist/202009/why-we-fear-death-and-how-overcome-it

WyattG. (2023, May 29). *Quick Reference Guide for Railroad Disability Medicare - Medicare Insurance AZ*. Medicare Insurance. https://www.medicareinsuranceaz.com/understanding-medicare-enrollment-periods

Zenhabits. (2022, April 2). *The Subtle Power of Changing Your Identity - zen habits*. Zen Habits. https://zenhabits.net/identity/

Zhihan, S., Mohammadiounotikandi, A., Khanlooei, S. G., Monjezi, S., Umaralievich, M. S., Ehsani, A. A., & Lee, S. (2023). A new conceptual model to investigate the role of hospital's capabilities on sustainable learning. *Heliyon, 9*(11), e20890. https://doi.org/10.1016/j.heliyon.2023.e20890

Zhou, J., Xiang, H., & Xie, B. (2022). Better safe than sorry: a study on older adults' credibility judgments and spreading of health misinformation. *Universal Access in the Information Society, 22*(3), 957–966. https://doi.org/10.1007/s10209-022-00899-3

Zhou, R., Cui, J., & Yin, X. (2023). Perceived family relationships and social participation through sports of urban older adults living alone: An analysis of the mediating effect of self-respect levels. *Frontiers in Public Health, 11*. https://doi.org/10.3389/fpubh.2023.1095302

Made in the USA
Middletown, DE
26 July 2025